Gammon *and* Spinach

Also by Simon Hopkinson

(with Lindsey Bareham)

Roast Chicken and Other Stories

The Prawn Cocktail Years

Simon Hopkinson

Gammon *and* Spinach

photographs by Jason Lowe

MACMILLAN

Dedicated to:

FRANCIS COULSON

4 June 1919 – 20 February 1998

First published 1998 by Macmillan

an imprint of Macmillan Publishers Ltd
25 Eccleston Place, London SW1W 9NF
and Basingstoke

Associated companies throughout the world

ISBN 0 333 73585 4

9 8 7 6 5 4 3 2 1

A CIP catalogue record for this book is available from the British Library.

Typeset by The Florence Group, Stoodleigh, Devon
Printed and bound in Italy by
New Interlitho

A frog he would a-wooing go,

    Heigh ho! says Rowley,

A frog he would a-wooing go,

Whether his mother would let him or no.

    With a rowley, powley, gammon and spinach,

    Heigh ho! says Anthony Rowley.

Anon.

Preface

When I was first approached to write a regular column for the *Independent*, all I could think of was how I could possibly, even in my wildest dreams, come up with anything close to the originator of the column, the late Jeremy Round.

I was fortunate enough to know Jeremy socially, together with his friend Jeremy Trevathan, for the last few years of his life. Although we only shared a few precious dinners together – plus one memorable Sunday lunch at Kensington Place which ran into dinner – his deep love of cooking, eating and all things culinary came over with such genuine pleasure that I knew this was a very special gourmet indeed. To be able to put this enthusiasm and ardour into his natural gift for writing seemed inevitable. His talent and friendship to many continues to be missed.

I hesitate to make any sort of comparison, but I guess there were some obvious similarities between us: the love of dining, the joy of cooking, a fanatical need to always eat the very, very best – whether it be beluga caviar or bubble and squeak – and, luckily, to have been given the opportunity to write about all these things. Now there the similarity ends, as he was simply quite brilliant at this and clearly loved doing his column. Well, I do too, in my own way.

When I decided to pack up my knives and apron and withdraw from the heat and bustle of the Bibendum kitchen (nearly four years ago now), I had tentatively started to write a little here and there. My very, very first, tiny weeny little effort was as a guest recipe columnist for Fay Maschler, when she was on holiday from presenting her regular 'Eating In' column for the *Evening Standard* (this was some time in 1985, I think). I was thrilled to be asked and really enjoyed this first flirtation with food journalism – and was paid rather well if I remember.

The surprising outcome of this was a charming letter from Anthony Goff, of the highly respectable David Higham and Associates, literary agents, suggesting that I might be interested in writing a book! Excuse me? Little me, a chef slaving away in the bowels of a small restaurant called Hilaire, in Old Brompton Road, South Kensington, SW7. Write a cookery book . . . ? Oh yeah, sure, why not. Nine years later, *Roast Chicken and Other Stories* was finally published.

I am indebted, thirteen years later, to know that Anthony Goff is still there, looking after my very best interests, always telling me that 'everything will all be all right'. So, too, does the redoubtable Jacqueline Korn, who once employed the mother of my erstwhile sous-chef Henry Harris (he rules over The Fifth Floor restaurant in Harvey Nichols), elder brother of Matthew, and who, for almost four years now, has been the chef at Bibendum.

But it was to be the canny Emily Green, the original (and remaining as the best) restaurant critic for the *Independent*, who gave me my first stab at writing the odd column for the *Indie*. She initially allowed me to list my ten favourite restaurants in Paris and why (canny, or what?) in one enjoyable scribble. There then followed another, where I bravely compared the tiny Parisian bistro Cartet, near République, with the great Bocuse in Lyon. That was fun (Cartet sort of won really, because I love it, but Bocuse was just whippy-woo too, you understand). A few years later, Emily did not forget me when a regular post came up at the paper, in December 1994. I jumped at it, with relish, and have enjoyed every minute ever since. This was a sincere kindness, and a much-needed push into the unknown.

I also owe a huge debt to Delia Smith, and her husband Michael Wynn-Jones, for asking me to be one of the original contributors to *Sainsbury's The Magazine*. This was to be my first very own monthly column in what turned out to be one of the most successful cookery magazines ever. The first issue hit the checkouts in May 1993 and was an immediate success up and down the land. It was wonderful to have been part of such an energetic and enthusiastic team right from the very beginning, urged on by editor Michael, and inspired by Delia's infectious ideas and no-nonsense approach to cookery. My final column went out last April, five years on, but a very important, happy and formative five years.

However, it was Jill Norman who finally gave me a shove towards writing my first book (that which was to be so long in writing), *Roast Chicken and Other Stories*. At one point I confessed to Jill that I feared that

I was not going to be able to finish it, the business of running Bibendum being foremost in my mind, coupled with the slowness of writing everything in long hand. Enter friend and seasoned cookery writer, Lindsey Bareham.

For it was Lindsey who suggested she help me to put the book together and so save me from imminent embarrassment. I scribbled a bit more, dictated too and was further guided by my friend as to how to put recipes together. We had a good time doing it too. This was so much the case, that when the idea of material that eventually became *The Prawn Cocktail Years* occurred to us (at the end of a long day's graft and over a bottle of Gewürtztraminer), we decided to do it again. And it was a pleasure.

But now, with this book, I am all alone. It should be accepted, I know, that this is a compilation of my articles gleaned from the *Independent* over the last three years, but there has been some serious stitching together, additional introductions and some wonderful new photographs from the very talented Mr Jason Lowe. And I should like to add here that a great deal of the pleasure I get from doing my column is much heightened by the regular photography sessions with Jason that take place in my kitchen here at home.

Much that I have managed to scribble over the past couple of years has been greatly enhanced by Allan Jenkins, my editor at the *Independent*. We agree so readily, so often, and about nearly everything, that he has almost become my alter ego. His enthusiasm over what good food should be has rarely been matched in my memory. He also pointed me in the right direction when I started to think about taking on two Burmese kittens. I sometimes curse him when they have shredded up the sixth roll of Andrex in a week, and then the next thing I'm doing is steaming them a chicken breast. So we talk about that too. A real treasure to know.

My other editorial muse is Georgina Morley (she likes cats too and also quite likes her new baby boy, Charlie). I knew immediately that George and I would get on famously, as her first few words to me in the lift at Macmillan Books included the four-letter one amongst them. Twice. She was an invaluable tower of strength whilst Lindsey and I worked on *The Prawn Cocktail Years*, and it was she who urged me to put this collection together over a jolly dinner at Le Caprice. And a big thank you too, to Catherine Whitaker, who looked after me whilst George looked after Charlie.

If you are a regular reader of the *Indie* every Saturday, then you will by now know a little about my views on food: the eating, the cooking, the buying, the all important seasons. Also my screeches about pretentiousness, the need to cook for pleasure rather than with a slavishness towards fashion and not to be taken in by some – but not all – of the unadulterated crap one sees on the television – supposedly in the name of 'good cooking'! Bring back Fanny is what I say!

If, however, the contents of this book are completely new to you, I hope that you will simply enjoy cooking some of the recipes you find here. Even if it is only one, so be it; better that, than the book sits on a coffee table gathering dust rather than the splashes of a busy kitchen.

Simon Hopkinson

London, February 1998

Recipes

Hot and Cold Soups

Oysters and Mussels

Salads

Potted and Cured Meats

Fish and Shellfish

Preserved Fish

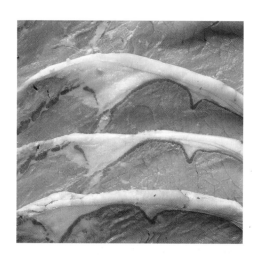

Meat

Poultry and Game

Offal

Vegetable Dishes

Rice and Pasta

Pastry

Puddings

Hot and Cold
Soups

Chicken Broth ‡

This simple broth is possibly the most useful liquid to have to hand in the kitchen. It is the easiest thing to make and simply requires putting several ingredients into a pot, adding liquid, bringing it to a simmer and cooking in a low oven for 2 hours. Once strained and divested of excess fat the broth is ready to use for endless soups and braises. It can also be further reduced to give a more intense flavour and used in sauces and to enrich casseroles. Freeze in pots for use at any time.

For making 2 litres of broth:
1 kg chicken wings (or failing that, drumsticks – still relatively cheap), roughly chopped
3 sticks celery, chopped
3 leeks, trimmed, chopped and washed
1 medium carrot, peeled and chopped
2 small onions, peeled and chopped
3 cloves garlic, bashed
4 ripe tomatoes, peeled and chopped
1 chicken stock cube
3 sprigs thyme
2 bay leaves
8 black peppercorns
6 sprigs parsley
3 litres water

Put all the ingredients for the broth into a large pan, bring up to a simmer, skim off any resultant froth and cook at the merest blip for 3 hours. Pour through a colander into a clean pan and leave to drain and drip for 15 minutes. Remove any fat from the surface with several sheets of absorbent kitchen paper. Gently reduce until there is approximately 2 litres of broth and strain through a fine sieve. Remove any further scum or fat, cool, and then ladle into 4 pots. Put lids on and freeze.

Note: To defrost, either use a microwave or tip straight into a pan and heat through over a low light.

Pea and Ham Soup ‡ serves 5–6

In effect, two recipes in one. I have always thought – and was taught to think, both by my mother and intelligent tutors – that good cooking is one-third talent, one-third skill and one-third good taste. But there is one further very important fraction missing: providence. I can buy two fresh ham hocks from Sid, my local butcher in Brook Green, West London, for a couple of quid or so. He will also chuck in a couple of trotters for a few more pence, to further enrich the cooking liquor. This will instantly make me think *jambon persillé*, or chopped jellied ham with parsley, knowing that the trotters will set the stock around the nuggets of ham.

When I invite folk in for supper it is often this sort of vehicle upon which the meal will revolve. This is not because the ingredients are cheap, but because they are delicious. I have been known to offer caviar followed by ham hocks, both being good to eat; the money saved on the hocks has allowed me to splash out on a treat. And treats are intended to be rare.

So when I have carefully simmered the hocks and trotters in just water, vegetables, herbs and appropriate spices, the resultant broth is there for me to make a split pea and ham soup of great quality, with enough of the liquid to make my jellied ham. It having cost almost next to nothing, I can then think about a couple of expensive fat ducks for the next main course. Then, of course, there is the duck broth I am going to make . . .

For the ham broth:

2 small ham hocks
2 small pig's trotters, split lengthways
   by the butcher (optional)
1–1.5 litres water
2 large leeks, trimmed, split and
   washed
2 sticks celery, halved
2 carrots, peeled and sliced lengthways
1 onion, peeled and stuck with
   3 cloves
2 bay leaves
a few peppercorns
1 small glass cider

Put the hocks (and trotters if using) in a roomy stewpan. Cover with cold water (not the given 1–1.5 litres), bring to the boil and discard the water. Refill with the measured water and tuck in the vegetables, bay leaves and peppercorns. Add the cider. Bring to the boil, remove any scum that forms on the surface and simmer extremely gently for 1½ hours. Discard the vegetables. Now carefully lift out the hocks (and trotters), remove skin and fat if you wish and pull the meat off the bone. Shred if using for soup; keep warm and in whole pieces if serving with parsley sauce. Pour the broth through a fine sieve and use as desired; there should be about 1 litre.

To make the soup:
75g butter
2 onions, peeled and chopped
2 cloves garlic, peeled and crushed
1 litre ham broth

200g green split peas
freshly ground white pepper
150ml whipping cream
2–3 tbsp shredded ham

Melt the butter in a pan and sweat the onions and garlic until soft and lightly coloured. Pour in the broth and add the peas. Bring to the boil, remove any scum that forms on the surface and simmer for about 1 hour, or until the peas are well cooked and soft. If the soup seems too thick, let it down with a little water. Liquidize, or, for a mealier texture, put the soup through a vegetable mill (*mouli-légumes*). Return to a clean pan and add some pepper and the cream. Gently reheat with the cooked ham, and serve.

Cream of Butter-bean Soup with Rosemary and Anchovy Butter   serves 4

At a pinch, this soup can be a success when made with tinned butter beans (drained and rinsed in a sieve); a useful addition to anyone's store cupboard. I am seldom averse to opening a tin of anything, just so long as the contents are worth it. Most canned pulses are dependable, as are other things that come in tins: chopped tomatoes, coconut milk, goose fat, anchovies, tiny tins of Clamato (for making big Bloody Marys) and Heinz tomato soup. If you do decide to make the soup using canned beans (3 x 400g tins, drained, should be sufficient), the soup will naturally not take as long to cook.

250g dried butter-beans
(Spanish ones are particularly fine)
75g butter
2 large onions, peeled and sliced
3 sticks celery, chopped
2 sprigs rosemary
1 litre water
freshly ground black pepper
1 chicken stock cube
Maldon sea salt

150ml whipping cream

For the rosemary and anchovy butter:
100g unsalted butter, softened
2 sprigs rosemary, leaves only
1 clove garlic, peeled and crushed
1 x 50g tin anchovies
juice of ½ a small lemon
freshly ground black pepper

Soak the beans in plenty of cold water overnight, or for at least 6 hours. Drain. In a roomy pan, melt the butter and fry the onions and celery until lightly coloured. Add the rosemary, stir around and allow its aroma to lift. Tip in the drained beans, add the measured water and bring up to a boil. Remove any scum that forms and then allow to simmer very, very gently, covered, for around 1½ hours or so, or until the beans are very soft and almost falling apart. Add pepper and the stock cube and simmer for a further 10 minutes. Check for seasoning. (*Note:* It is important not to season until this stage, as salt included during the cooking of the beans can sometimes result in them developing tough skins, but also remember that anchovy butter is added later.)

Meanwhile, make the rosemary and anchovy butter by combining all the ingredients together in a food processor until very smooth. Pass through a small sieve to remove any spiky rosemary bits. Tip into a small bowl and leave at room temperature until the soup is to be served.

Lift out the rosemary sprigs and then put the beans, vegetables and liquor into a liquidizer and process until very smooth. Pour through a sieve into a clean pan, stir in the cream and keep hot.

To serve, pour into large soup plates or bowls, drop a spoonful of the rosemary and anchovy butter into each and serve with croutons.

Warm and Sloppy Green Summer Vegetable Soup ‡ serves 6

There is nothing nicer, when celebrating prime summer vegetables, than to leave them to themselves. And in essence, that is what this soup is all about. In smart restaurants my particular chosen whimsical moniker might possibly be given the misnomer 'ragout'. Well it isn't that at all. It's a slop. But very delicious slop.

50g butter
450g courgettes, peeled and cut into
  small chunks (not diced)
250g cucumber, peeled and cut into
  small chunks (not diced)
450g fresh peas, podded (keep the
  pods)
1 litre vegetable stock (the Swiss
  powdered vegetable stock called
  'Marigold' is perfect here)
1 kg broad beans, podded and then
  blanched in boiling water, skins
  slipped off with your fingers

350g new potatoes, peeled and cut into
  small chunks
1 cos lettuce, trimmed of outside
  dark green leaves and then
  shredded
10g spring onions, trimmed and finely
  chopped (don't add too much of the
  green parts)
Maldon sea salt and freshly ground
  black pepper
2 level tbsp chopped mint
6 tsp white wine vinegar

Melt the butter in a roomy pot and gently sweat the courgettes and cucumber until soft. Meanwhile, coarsely chop the pea pods and add to the stock. Allow to boil for about 15 minutes and then strain into the courgettes and cucumber. Discard the pods. Add the beans, peas and potato and bring to a simmer. Cook for about 20 minutes and then incorporate the lettuce and spring onions. Check for seasoning and cook for a further 5 minutes. Stir the mint into the soup. Remove from the heat, cover, and allow to cool to lukewarm before eating. Dribble a teaspoon of good quality white wine vinegar over each serving.

Caldo Verde ⁝ serves 8

In Portugal, the cabbage used is one called *couve gallego*. Use kale or Savoy cabbage to replicate the real thing. Incidentally, the Italian cabbage *cavolo nero*, now a little more available here, might be just the ticket. Whatever you decide to use, however, do try to shred it as finely as you dare (do not be tempted to use a food processor, as it tears and destroys the fibres of the cabbage). On a personal note, I love the soup without the traditional addition of some sliced garlic sausage. If you prefer to add this, introduce it at the same time as you put in the cabbage. This fine recipe is based upon the one found in *The Food of Portugal* by Jean Anderson (Hearst Books, New York, 1986).

4 tbsp olive oil
1 large onion, peeled and finely
   chopped
1 large clove garlic, peeled and finely
   chopped
6 large floury potatoes, peeled and
   chopped

2.3 litres cold water
175g sliced garlic sausage such as
   chorizo (optional)
2½ tsp salt
plenty of freshly ground black pepper
450g cabbage leaves, trimmed of coarse
   stems and hand sliced filament-thin

Heat 2 tbsp of the oil and sauté the onion and garlic for a couple of minutes, until they begin to colour slightly. Add the potatoes and pour on the water. Cook gently, at a simmer, until the potatoes collapse (we say 'lobbed' in Lancashire). Meanwhile, and if using, fry the sausage over a low heat in 1 tbsp of the oil until most of the fat has run out. Drain on kitchen paper for a minute or two.

Ladle by ladle, work the potato broth through a vegetable mill (*mouli-légumes*) into a clean pan. Add the sausage, salt, pepper and cabbage, and return to the heat, simmering for anything between 5 and 10 minutes, until the cabbage is tender. Check for seasoning and stir in the last of the olive oil. Serve in large soup plates with good bread such as thick slices of toasted sourdough.

The finest fish soup can only be made from the finest fish. That is not to say that a perfectly acceptable and delicious fish soup cannot also be made from fishbones, a bag of mussels, a few chopped-up vegetables and a degree of nous.

Culinary squabbles over what constitutes a proper fish soup are legion. The very name conjures up all sorts of romance: fishing boats bobbing about by the harbour walls of the old port of Marseilles, housing gnarled and weather-beaten fishermen with rich accents peppered by local patois. But it is which are the *only* fish that can be used in a true fish soup that causes the most dispute.

Mullet, they say, is indispensable, *rascasse* and John Dory too. The horribly dull to the eye, yet poisonously finned, weaver fish is – so we are told – the most important creature of all for inclusion. A generous cross-section of conger eel should be in there too, to provide richness and body to the broth, as, supposedly, do clumps of bland monkfish in some kitchens.

Many stellar chefs, these days, insist that the basic broth of the soup should be fashioned from a fish stock that is already to hand: 'Take two pints of fish stock, etc. (see page 752)' is a typical instruction in some of the more complicated manuals. Try explaining that to one of those gnarled Marseilles fishermen, wearing his stripy T-shirt and exhaling well-used breath between puffs of his Disque Bleu.

Perhaps those old fish soups made on board whilst anchored in a local maritime port never tasted as good as the ones you might now carefully make upon the halogen glow of your latest Smeg. But be assured, they will all have – at one time or another – tasted wonderful, good, really quite nice, average and, frankly, vile. But different and certainly individual. How was it for you, when you last made your fish soup in a small dinghy on the Norfolk Broads?

The following recipe certainly worked for me, but you can almost use any fish you like, although oily fish such as salmon, and herrings or mackerel, are not brilliant.

100 ml pure olive oil (not extra-virgin)

1 tbsp tomato purée

5 large leeks, trimmed and sliced, then
    washed

1 whole head of garlic, cloves
    separated, peeled and crushed

4 sticks celery, chopped

1 large bulb fennel, chopped

1.4–1.8 kg mixed Mediterranean
    fish, cut into chunks

a good slug of Pernod or Ricard

½ bottle dry white wine

2.3 litres water

6 strips orange peel

1 tsp (or less) dried chilli flakes

1 generous tsp saffron threads

a few sprigs of thyme

2 bay leaves

1 star anise, crushed

10 ripe tomatoes, peeled and chopped

Maldon sea salt

For the rouille:

This is the essential spiced garlic emulsion that lifts the soup into a class act. Serve it separately in a bowl, at table, for people to add as much as they wish and then stir in, or spread upon the croutons.

2 hard-boiled egg yolks

2 uncooked egg yolks

½ tsp saffron threads, steeped in
    1 tbsp hot water for 5 minutes

3 anchovy fillets

1 garlic clove, peeled and crushed

1 tsp tomato purée

1 tsp Dijon mustard

a little Maldon sea salt

a squeeze of lemon juice

several drops of Tabasco

250 ml virgin olive oil

Heat the olive oil gently in a roomy pan and add the tomato purée. Fry carefully over a low heat until the purée has become rust coloured. Now add the leeks, garlic, celery and fennel. Stew gently until coloured – about 10 minutes. Tip in the fish and turn the heat up slightly. Stir around until the fish is starting to break up somewhat, turn up the heat and then slosh in the Pernod or Ricard and set light to it. Once the flames have died down, pour in the wine and top up with the water. Add the rest of the ingredients and stir well. Slowly bring up to a simmer and then start to skim the froth from the surface, which will appear in copious amounts. Simmer gently for 1 hour, stirring occasionally.

Now tip the whole lot into a spacious colander suspended over a clean pan. Allow to drip for at least 10 minutes, then press and push the mulchy mess around the colander so that as much as possible of the flavour left in the fish can be transferred to the soup below. Discard the mulch and then pass the soup through a reasonably fine sieve into another vessel. Allow to stand for a few minutes and then remove excess oil from the surface with several sheets of kitchen paper; don't remove it all, since a nice sheen of oil is one of the characteristics of this soup.

The soup now needs some reduction to intensify its flavour. Simmer down gently, skimming any impurities as you go, until the flavour is good and full flavoured (you should end up with around 1.5 litres).

To make the rouille, purée the first 10 ingredients until smooth in a food processor. Add the oil in a thin stream, until the rouille is thoroughly homogenized.

To serve the soup, check the seasoning, pour into a handsome tureen or bowl and serve with croutons (made from a small baguette that has been well rubbed with a clove of garlic, sliced into discs and dried out in a low oven until crisp) and the rouille. I am not a fan of the traditional grated Gruyère cheese that is often served as well; I don't find cheese and fish compatible.

The Oriental Hotel's Sea Crab Soup with Coconut Milk ‡ serves 4

I ate this extraordinary soup, *Tom Gathi Poo Khai*, whilst staying at the Oriental Hotel in Bangkok earlier this year. It is, without doubt, one of the most glorious fish soups I can ever remember eating. If you are very lucky, like me, to live in west London, the Thai ingredients for this wonderful soup may be purchased from a shop called Sri Thai, in Shepherd's Bush Road (the Bush end). Otherwise, search out your nearest Asian store. Note: unless you know how to kill a live crab, it is worth asking the fishmonger to do it for you. Once dispatched, however, the crabs must be cooked as soon as possible.

2 × 400g tins coconut milk
2 small live female crabs, first boiled
*   for 2 minutes, to kill them*

3 tbsp peeled and sliced Thai pink
*   shallots*
6–8 slices of galangal ginger

Right: **The Oriental Hotel's Sea Crab Soup with Coconut Milk**

5–6 kaffir lime leaves, sliced

5–6 small hot red chillies, sliced
(deseeded if you wish)

3 stalks of lemon grass, sliced
(only use the 5 cm bulbous part of
the stalks)

4–5 tbsp Thai fish sauce

4–5 tbsp lime juice

1 x 250g packet of creamed
coconut, chopped into small
chunks

1 heaped tbsp coarsely chopped
coriander leaves

1 large mild red chilli, sliced
(optional)

a little chilli oil (optional)

Bring the coconut milk to a simmer in a roomy pot and lower in the crabs. Return to a simmer, put a lid on and cook gently for 15 minutes. Lift out the crabs and allow to cool. Add the shallots, galangal ginger, lime leaves, hot red chillies and lemon grass. Add the creamed coconut and simmer for a further 5 minutes. Switch off the heat while you deal with the crabs.

Break open the cooled crabs by pulling apart the body of the crab from its outer shell. Remove the grey-looking 'dead man's fingers', scoop out the brown meat from the shell and put it onto a plate. Discard the shell. Now remove the large claws and give them a sharp crack with a rolling pin. Chop the body of the crab in half (which includes the remaining lesser claws) and put all the crab and brown meat (including any escaped juices) back into the soup. Bring back to a simmer, add the coriander, and mild chilli and chilli oil, if using. Cook for a further 5 minutes and serve piping hot.

Spinach Soup with Lemon ⸭ serves 4–5

You can't add lemon juice to spinach. Well, you can, but it will simply turn out as dingy grey as a pair of Popeye's Y-fronts. The acidity of the juice also destroys the structure of the vegetable, causing it to become slimy and almost curdled in appearance. This is just fine for when you are braising lamb in the Greek fashion, when the meat is slowly stewed for a few sunny hours with spinach and much lemon juice, and becomes slippery and fragrant and simultaneously tenderizes the meat until it almost melts.

But the beauty of this verdant soup is its colour and freshness of flavour.

The lemon juice is gently carried into the soup by a wave of acidulated cream spooned onto its surface.

50g butter

4 small leeks, most of the green part
  removed, sliced and washed

2 cloves garlic, peeled and
  crushed

700ml light chicken stock

750g washed and dried spinach leaves
  (the ready packed bags from supermarkets are ideal here)

1 small bunch flat-leaf parsley, leaves
  only

Maldon sea salt and freshly ground
  black pepper

150ml whipping cream

juice of ½ a lemon

1 small lemon, skin and pith removed
  and cut into thin slices, picking out
  any stray seeds

Melt the butter in a roomy pan and sweat the leeks until really soft. Add the garlic and cook a little longer. Pour in the stock and bring to the boil. Simmer for 10 minutes and then tip in the spinach and parsley, and season. Cook for a further 10 minutes and then purée, in batches, in the liquidizer until very smooth. Pass through a sieve into a clean pan and gently reheat. Check the seasoning.

Just before serving, quickly mix the cream and lemon juice together until smooth. Pour the soup into individual bowls and swirl the cream over the surface. Float the lemon slices on top and serve.

Chilled Sorrel Soup   ‡   serves 4

This is a light and creamy soup, naturally sharp and refreshing. With reference to 'Spinach Soup with Lemon', don't now be upset that the sorrel quickly turns a muddy green colour when cooked. It can't help it; sorrel is made that way.

Many years ago I employed a particularly pedantic chef, who was obsessed with how things looked, almost more than with anything else (I seem to remember he had worked in the Terrace Restaurant of the Dorchester before coming to me). He was a good cook, but would become very frustrated indeed when his perfect strips of freshly snipped sorrel leaves turned a muddy green, almost on contact, when stirred into his masterly cream sauce, served with his immaculately trimmed rectangle of salmon fillet.

900ml light chicken stock, reserving 150ml for cooking the sorrel
6 egg yolks
275ml whipping cream
Maldon sea salt and white pepper

450g sorrel, stalks removed, veined and coarsely chopped
juice of ½ a lemon
finely chopped chives or chervil

Bring the stock to the boil in a roomy pan, then turn down to the merest simmer. Whisk together the egg yolks and cream. Now, wash the whisk and start to gently move it through the stock in a circular motion. At a regular pace, whisk the stock and at the same time add the egg and cream liaison in a thin stream. Let the soup cook *very* gently, stirring with a wooden spoon as if making custard. But, like custard, it can easily curdle, so watch out. The result should be limpid, smooth and the consistency of thin cream. Immediately remove from the heat and liquidize. Pour into a china or stainless-steel bowl.

Now bring the reserved stock to the boil in a non-reactive (stainless-steel or enamelled) pan, then add the sorrel and briefly cook until thoroughly wilted. Add to the soup and stir in well, together with the lemon juice. Cool and then chill in the fridge for at least 4 hours. Ladle into chilled bowls and sprinkle over the chives or chervil.

Tomato Consommé ‡ serves 4

This pale elixir can be eaten either hot or cold; if the latter, you may like to gel the consommé by the addition of a few leaves of gelatine. It naturally should not be a stiff jelly, rather a trembling bowlful. A spoonful of crème fraiche, further sharpened by lemon juice and perfumed with fresh basil leaves, is a special addition to the jellied version too. It is essential to use a stainless-steel or other non-reactive saucepan here.

Right: **Tomato Consommé**

*3 kg very ripe tomatoes — it is not
  worth making the consommé if
  they are not*
3 cloves garlic, peeled and sliced
a little Maldon sea salt

a large pinch of dried red chilli flakes
*1 large bunch of basil — and I mean
  large*
2 leaves gelatine (optional)

Peel the tomatoes by plunging into boiling water for 15 seconds and immediately draining. With a small knife, cut and slice them any how directly into the pan, so as not to waste any precious juices. Put in the garlic, salt and chilli and set on a low light. Bring up to a simmer, stir and put on a lid. The liquid that forms comes purely from the tomatoes. Cook for 40 minutes. Tear in the basil leaves and continue simmering for a further 10 minutes. Strain through a colander into a clean bowl or other pan. Leave to drip for a good hour, but do not force the pulp (use the pulp for another dish). At this point, if you wish to gel the consommé, soften the gelatine in cold water. Squeeze dry and warm through in a small pan with a little of the tomato liquid, to melt it, then stir back in.

Now, using a damp tea towel or a jelly bag, further strain the tomato liquid into another, scrupulously clean bowl. It is best to support it well above the container (jelly bags usually have strings attached so that they can be hooked up). Allow to drip until it stops completely. The liquid should settle in the bowl and be clear. However, if there is a little settlement at the bottom, simply pour off the clear liquid into another container.

Zuppa Cuata ✣ serves 4

If I had not read a charming article on Sardinia, lovingly written by food writer Phillipa Davenport (she is a huge fan of the island) during the early part of 1996, then I would have known nothing about Saltara. It is one of those *agri-tourismo* farmhouse restaurants in the north of the island near Santa Theresa di Gallura — and a fine example it is, to be sure (if you ever have the opportunity to make a visit — which you should — the telephone number is 0039 789 755597).

Phillipa wrote: 'At Saltara, hams, sausages and other pork products are raised, killed and cured on the premises. Natalia Varsi makes her own cheese and breads, baking the latter in the outdoor ovens in which her husband roasts meats, the juices of which drip onto dishes of potatoes grown by her father and scattered with herbs from the wild.'

The farm is set in dramatic craggy scenery, seemingly in the middle of nowhere. We watched the sun slip away behind a jagged line of rocky terrain as a wooden platter of home-made salami, pancetta (particularly fine) and *coppa* were brought to the table. Balanced upon this was a further board covered with wafer-thin slices of milky cheese (made the day before), scattered with herbs and slicked with olive oil. Silence settled with sundown as we greedily ate.

However, the dish that deeply settled in my memory almost more than anything else, was the *zuppa cuata*: 'lost, or hidden soup'. It was simply a broth (or even just water on occasion) that is baked in the oven with broken up pieces of stale country bread, mixed with some tomatoes and basil, and finished with some of their own farm cheese. The bread soaks up, or 'hides' the liquid in itself, as it cooks. The quintessential late supper, after having enjoyed a lazy summer lunch in the garden.

8 very ripe large tomatoes, skinned and
   coarsely chopped, or 1 x 400g can
   chopped tomatoes
2 cloves garlic, chopped
4 tbsp good olive oil
a pinch of dried chilli
Maldon sea salt

150g country bread, torn into
   chunks
12 leaves of basil
400ml light meat or poultry
   broth
50g grated pecorino sardo *or*
   Parmesan

Preheat the oven to 400°F/205°C/gas mark 6.

Put the tomatoes, garlic, 1 tbsp of oil, chilli and a little salt into a heavy-bottomed saucepan. Reduce to a thick sauce over gentle heat – about 20 minutes. Meanwhile, put the bread into a deep oven dish, tuck in the basil leaves and pour over the broth. Allow the broth to be completely 'lost' into the bread, which should be ready by the time the tomatoes have reduced. Spread the tomatoes over the bread and scatter thickly with the *pecorino* or Parmesan. Spoon over the remaining olive oil and put in the oven for 20 minutes. Finally, heat an overhead grill to full and burnish the cheesy surface to a bubbling, crusted brown. Leave to cool to lukewarm before eating with crisp lettuce and a sharp dressing.

Joan Stirling's Cold Curried Apple Soup ‡ serves 4

I first came across this exceptionally good cold soup whilst working at the Hat and Feather restaurant in Knutsford, Cheshire, some twenty years ago now. Some may think it sounds odd and, how shall one say, rather dated? But it is a rare combination; sweet yet savoury, elusive, seductive and perfectly English.

25g butter
1 onion, peeled and chopped
1 tbsp Madras curry powder
900 ml light chicken stock (I have made it very successfully using cubes)
450g dessert apples and 450g Granny Smith apples, peeled,
cored, and chopped
Maldon sea salt
juice of ½ a large and juicy lemon, or more if a sharper-tasting soup is desired
200 ml whipping cream
chopped mint (apple mint is best)
cayenne pepper

Melt the butter in a roomy pan and fry the onion gently until pale golden. Add the curry powder and cook over a very gentle heat for a couple of minutes. Pour in the stock, bring to the boil and add the apples and a little salt. Turn down to a simmer and cook for about 30 minutes, stirring occasionally; the apples must be completely soft and pulpy. Liquidize in batches until very smooth and pass through a fine sieve. Allow to cool, stir in the lemon juice and whisk in the cream. Check for seasoning and chill well in the fridge. Pour into cold soup bowls, sprinkle with chopped mint and dust with a little cayenne pepper.

Oysters *and* Mussels

Mussels with Cream, Tarragon and Poached Egg ‡ serves 4

I really love little shelled mussel dishes such as this one here. It is a surprisingly sophisticated first course and would happily grace the table of the most discerning dinner party. You might well look upon the chore of shucking the mussels as a tedious bore. Well, if that's the case, read no further.

But listen, cookery isn't all 'simplicity itself', or 'something easy for a last-minute supper after a hard day at the office'. It also just happens to be an interesting thing to do for some folk, as it can be an enormous pleasure and satisfying pastime. I do sometimes wonder why people who never seem to enjoy cooking much will always have a copy of *The Joy of Cookery* (usually a pristine copy) on their kitchen bookshelf, rather than *Fifty Easy Ways with Pasta* – or some such pamphlet.

Note: The kneaded butter used in this recipe is a very useful thing to have around. Stored in a pot in the fridge it will keep for a week or so. Simply mix together equal quantities (say 100 g) of soft butter and flour to a paste; it's really just an uncooked roux.

50 g butter
1 medium onion, finely chopped
2 tbsp tarragon vinegar
150 ml dry white wine
1 kg mussels, cleaned and
    bearded
1 tsp kneaded butter (beurre manié)

150 ml double cream
freshly ground white pepper
4 eggs
4 slices bread, cut from a large baguette
    and fried in butter until crisp
4 sprigs tarragon, leaves only, finely
    chopped

Take a very large pan with a lid. Melt the butter and fry the onion until soft and transparent, then add the vinegar. Reduce it to nothing and then add the white wine. Allow it to bubble for a couple of minutes and then tip in the mussels. Once they are cooked (opened), strain through a colander into another pan or bowl. Allow the mussels to drain off all their liquid and then strain their cooking juices once more through a fine sieve into a medium-sized saucepan. Shell the mussels (checking for any remaining stubborn beards and discarding any closed ones), put onto a plate and set on one side. Now start to add the kneaded butter to the saucepan, whisking as you go, and allow to simmer and thicken for a good five minutes. Add the cream and simmer once more for a moment or two. Check for seasoning and add the pepper if needed.

To assemble, poach the eggs in the usual way, drain onto folded kitchen paper and then place each one onto the pieces of fried bread in shallow soup plates. Add the tarragon to the sauce and tip in the mussels to heat through. Spoon over the eggs and bread and serve without delay.

Cream of Mussel Soup ‡ serves 4

One of the very nicest of fishy soups. The legendary Maxim's of Paris, in the Rue Royale, served – and possibly still does – a creamed mussel soup called *Potage Billy By*. I have looked through countless books to find an origin for this, alas without success. However, the recipe that I finally found for it (in a Papermac publication called *Secrets of the Great French Restaurants*, compiled by Louisette Bertholle in 1972) seems unusual, in that it simply uses the strained juices from cooking the mussels with wine, fish stock, onions, parsley and celery, which is then strained and cream added. But there is no mention of reintroducing the mussels, and this seems a pity. I have to say that the following recipe might be a little more substantial – and, if I may be so bold – somewhat more interesting than the Maxim's mode with mussel soup.

1.5 kg mussels, cleaned and bearded
150 ml medium dry white wine
  (Alsace is good here; drink the rest)
400 ml light chicken or fish stock
2 fat leeks, white part only, sliced and
  washed
1 fennel bulb, chopped

75 g butter
1 tbsp plain flour
½ tsp saffron
Maldon sea salt and freshly ground
  black pepper
150 ml whipping cream
1 level tbsp chopped tarragon

Put the mussels into a roomy pan and pour over the wine. Put a lid on and bring to the boil, shaking and stirring the mussels as you go. When you see that they have opened (the cooking process should not take much longer than about 5 minutes), drain into a colander suspended over another pan or bowl. Discard any closed ones. Shake the colander to get out any remaining liquor and then shell the mussels, putting the meat into a small bowl. Discard the shells and decant the mussel liquor through a double sheet of muslin into another pan together with the stock. Heat it up.

Wipe out the mussel pan and sweat the leeks and fennel in the butter until soft and golden. Stir in the flour and allow it to cook gently for a couple of minutes. Add the hot mussel liquor and stock mixture and stir until lightly thickened. Simmer for 20 minutes. Liquidize and then pass through a fine sieve back into the stock pan. Add the saffron, check the seasoning – you should not need much salt – and stir in the cream and tarragon. Tip in the shelled mussels, reheat fully, and serve.

Oysters Rockefeller ‡ serves 6

Last year, I read a recipe for oysters Rockefeller in a highly respectable journal, and it really made me quite cross. It was suggested, simply, that you were to chop a handful of spinach and three sprigs of parsley together, cover a dozen oysters with this mixture, and bake in a hot oven for 4–5 minutes. It was further pointed out that the oysters should not be over-cooked, but they should be hot, and that both the spinach and oysters should retain their texture.

Now if you are already a dab hand at cooking oysters, then you must already be a fairly knowledgeable cook. Thus you are also aware that raw spinach throws out the most embarrassing amount of water when heat is applied. I may, of course, have been misled here: perhaps the handful of spinach in question should have been previously cooked? However, it didn't say, so I am no wiser than you. But as the texture of the spinach was to be retained as it cooked, it suggests that this was not the case.

Right: **Oysters Rockefeller**

These points, it must be said, are almost irrelevant, because the dish described there (apart from the inclusion of spinach and parsley) has nothing whatsoever to do with the dish known as oysters Rockefeller. It will simply emerge looking quite horrid, taste of hardly anything at all, and the spinach will be scorched and dulled by intense heat from the oven.

Oysters Rockefeller was created at Antoine's restaurant in New Orleans almost 100 years ago – 1899, to be precise. I ate it there nearly four years ago and found it a poor dish, although I am sure this was not the case originally. Properly made, it is one of the greatest – if not the greatest – hot oyster dish ever created. Perhaps increasingly sloppy cooking over the years, catering to too many tourists who don't care, has taken its toll on an inspired recipe. There may have been minuscule changes to the original too – a form of gastronomic Chinese whispers at work, maybe.

The following recipe for the Rockefeller oyster mixture, however, is quite brilliant. It was given to me by Gay Bilson, who used to run the Bennelong restaurant within the Sydney Opera House. As you will see, it requires a little more work than simply flinging some chopped spinach and parsley over a few oysters. The Pernod and the celery, particularly, are essential to the mixture, as is the generous quantity of butter, which coheres and enriches this exquisite green purée.

It is preferable to purchase rock oysters for the dish, as the shells are good and deep and will accommodate the purée comfortably. If you are a dab hand at shucking oysters, then so do. Alternatively, ask your friendly fishmonger to do it for you and then hurry home. (Loch Fyne are perfect for this and they do mail order, but naturally un-shucked.)

Note: Make sure you ask him to also cut the muscle that secures the oyster to its shell, for ease of eating once covered with the topping.

36 rock oysters, shucked

For the Rockefeller purée:
700g spinach
25g parsley, leaves only, preferably the
  flat-leaf variety
275g unsalted butter

75g celery, finely chopped
50g shallots, peeled and chopped
50ml Pernod
several sprigs tarragon, leaves only
1 tsp Tabasco
1 level tsp Maldon sea salt
a handful of fresh breadcrumbs

Fill a very large pan with water and bring to the boil. Plunge in the spinach and parsley, allow to just about return to boiling point and then drain in a colander. Immediately refresh under very cold running water until completely cold. Squeeze as dry as possible between both hands until no more liquid seeps out; do this in small batches for maximum wringing. Set aside. Melt the butter in a deep frying pan (I know it seems an alarming amount, but fret not) and in it very gently fry the celery and shallots until softened – they will almost simmer in this copious amount of butter. Tip the contents of the frying pan into the goblet of a liquidizer. Put the pan back onto a moderate heat, pour in the Pernod and allow to warm through, but not to ignite. Add this to the liquidizer also. Now add the cooked spinach, tarragon, Tabasco and salt. Purée until very smooth and then push through a sieve into a bowl.

Preheat the oven to 450°F/230°C/gas mark 8.

Tip off any excess juice from the opened oysters (or drink it), and using a teaspoon completely cover each oyster with a generous coating of the green purée and place in a large, flat roasting tray (it can be advantageous to thickly strew the tray with some coarse rock salt, so as to allow the oysters to sit neatly and flat). Now carefully distribute a very fine showering of breadcrumbs over the oysters – it matters not a jot that some fall on salty ground – and put into the oven on the topmost shelf. Bake for about 8–10 minutes, or until the breadcrumbs are lightly toasted. Serve without delay and with some lemons to squeeze judiciously over each. My Australian friend came up with the very neat idea of putting Pernod in a spray bottle and giving the oysters a last-minute misting just before serving. This is an optional idea, but a masterly stroke of intelligent cookery.

Oysters Baked in Baguettes with Garlic Butter ‡ serves 4

This buttery feast is good for a feast around the kitchen table with a few bottles of Muscadet or Sançerre, rather than being part of a meal. Although I have never been lucky enough to eat the famous Oyster Po-Boy – a buttery oyster sandwich eaten as street food in New Orleans – this version will I hope bring back some memories to those who have.

1 long baguette
24 large rock oysters, shucked
lemon quarters

For the garlic butter:
225g butter, softened to room
   temperature
3 cloves garlic, crushed to a paste
   with a little Maldon sea salt

a handful of parsley leaves, finely
   chopped
a generous shake of Tabasco
Maldon sea salt and freshly ground
   black pepper to taste
1 dsp Pernod

Cut the baguette into 4 equal lengths, slicing off its very end knobs. Cut each length in half lengthways. Scrape out a little of the soft insides with a spoon; make this into breadcrumbs in a coffee grinder and lay on a tray to dry out.

Preheat the oven to 400°F/205°C/gas mark 6.

Lift the oysters out of their bottom shells and tip into a bowl together with any juices. One by one, lift them out and gently rinse under a cold tap (this ensures removal of any stray bits of shell). Put the oysters into a clean container and strain over the juices through a fine sieve. Whisk together the ingredients for the butter.

Into each of the 8 baguette 'boats' spread a little of the garlic butter – a smear, no more. Then cover with three oysters. Spoon a tiny amount of their liquor over each and sprinkle with the breadcrumbs. Dot each oyster with a scant teaspoon more of the garlic butter and place on a baking tray that has been strewn with coarse rock salt (this helps to prevent the bread from falling on its side). Bake in the top of the oven for 10–15 minutes or until the edges of the baguettes are golden brown, the butter melted and the oysters plumped up and breadcrumbs gilded. Serve with a little lemon squeezed over the oysters.

Deep-Fried Oysters and Onion Rings with Vietnamese Dipping Sauce ‡ serves 4

This is a dish that, over the years, gradually developed from a clear oyster soup that I once ate at the restaurant Kensington Place, in Notting Hill Gate, London. I so loved the combination of just-cooked oysters and almost raw onion rings, which floated in a beef consommé (itself an inspired carrying vehicle), that I just knew it could be a winner when deep fried with an Asian label attached; a sort of tempura with Vietnamese overtones. It has since made a regular appearance on the menu at Bibendum.

24 large rock oysters, shucked
a pinch of cayenne pepper
2 tbsp plain flour
2 small eggs, beaten
75 g fresh white breadcrumbs
2 medium onions, peeled and sliced
  into rings

For the Vietnamese dipping sauce:
1 small bunch of coriander, leaves only
12–15 mint leaves
2 cloves garlic, peeled and crushed
3 small green chillies, deseeded and
  chopped
2 tsp sugar
juice of 3 limes
*5 tbsp Thai fish sauce (*nam pla*)*
5 tbsp water

Lift the oysters out of their bottom shells and tip into a clean container together with any juices. One by one, lift them out and gently rinse under a cold tap (this ensures removal of any stray bits of shell). Put the oysters into a small pan and strain over the juices through a fine sieve. Heat very gently, swirling the pan around, until the oysters just start to take on a plumped look. Drain immediately and lay on kitchen paper to dry and cool quickly.

Begin to heat the oil in a deep fryer or chip basket to 350°F/180°C (for those without a deep fryer or thermometer, this is when a scrap of bread turns golden after a couple of minutes). Meanwhile, season the oysters with the cayenne, roll them in flour, then into egg and finally through the breadcrumbs. Try to be as deft as you can with this process: the less claggy the coating of the oysters, the finer will be the result. Do exactly the same to the onion rings.

Fry the onion rings first, until crisp and golden, then lay onto kitchen paper and keep warm in a low oven with the door ajar. Once the onions are cooked do the same with the oysters. For both items, cooking time will be 1–2 minutes.

Note: Do not overcrowd the fryer or pan, and also make sure that you bring the temperature back up before cooking the next batch of ingredients. To make the dipping sauce, work all the ingredients together in a food processor until well amalgamated but not a complete purée.

Warm Salad of Broad Beans, Bacon and Spinach ‡ serves 4

This is the perfect vegetable salad to make after the first of the young summer broad beans have passed their blush of youth. When freshly picked broad beans are such, there is no reason to divest them of their little pale green jackets, as they are as tender as can be. I have never understood why some of the more pretentious restaurants skin the most diminutive beans – even when no more than the size of a baby's fingernail. This is a big-boy bean salad, savoury and filling.

4 handfuls small, young and very fresh spinach leaves, washed and drained
10–12 very thin slices rindless streaky bacon, grilled until very crisp and brittle when cooled
2 sprigs tarragon, leaves only
6–8 sprigs flat-leafed parsley, leaves only
1 slice of white bread from a large loaf, cut into small cubes and fried in olive oil to make croutons

1.4–1.8 kg butch broad beans, podded
4–5 tbsp virgin olive oil
1 small clove garlic, peeled and finely chopped
1 small lemon, halved
1 large shallot, peeled and finely chopped
coarsely ground black pepper
a little flaky Maldon sea salt

Have a pan of well-salted boiling water on the go.

Take an attractive shallow white dish and strew it with the spinach leaves in a single layer. Break up the bacon into small pieces and scatter over the spinach. Now strew with the tarragon and parsley, so too with the croutons. Tip the beans into the boiling water. Boil fiercely for 2–3 minutes. Drain well and, whilst still warm, squeeze between thumb and first finger so that the inner bright green bean halves pop out. Evenly distribute over the spinach. Mix together the olive oil and garlic in a small bowl and spoon over the salad. Squeeze the lemon halves over everything and season with the shallot, pepper and a little salt. Serve immediately, but only toss the salad once it has reached the table.

Fennel Salad with Lemon and Olive Oil ‡ serves 4

This sharp and aromatic salad is particularly good as an accompaniment to grilled fish. It is important that the fennel is extremely fresh and that you do your best to slice it as thinly as possible. A scattering of fennel seeds, briefly toasted (in a dry frying pan until fragrant), will add sparkle, but this is an optional suggestion.

4 small very fresh bulbs of fennel,
*   trimmed and thinly sliced, any*
*   fronds reserved*
Maldon sea salt and freshly ground
*   black pepper*

juice of 1 lemon
2 tsp Pernod
4 tbsp extra-virgin olive oil

Lay out the fennel in a large shallow dish so that it is almost in a single layer. Season and sprinkle over the lemon juice and Pernod. Leave to macerate in a cool place for about 1 hour. Stir together briefly and once more lay out the slices of fennel; they will now have softened up somewhat. Spoon over the olive oil (if there were any sprightly fronds of green attached to the fennel bulbs, chop them up and sprinkle over the surface). Serve.

Tarragon Cream Dressing ‡ makes about 400 ml

In the early 1970s I worked in a fine restaurant called the Hat and Feather in Knutsford, Cheshire. Mrs Stirling – my employer, fine cook and muse – introduced me to this curious creamy salad dressing. More than anything else, it is, perhaps, closest to an old-fashioned English cooked salad cream, and there is that essential sweet and sour quality about it that appeals to all. Even though it contains eggs and vinegar, it bears no relation whatsoever to Continental mayonnaise or even a thickened vinaigrette.

The first time I encountered the dressing, it was spooned over a poached pear and served up as a first course. I have also seen it used with melon too. I promise you, it's really quite nice once you get used to the juxtaposition of flavours! Should you, however, not be keen on this rare school of mixing fruit with salad cream, then spoon it over cold chicken and hot new potatoes, and serve as a salad with crisp cos lettuce leaves. It's just fab.

2 large eggs	*5 tbsp good quality tarragon vinegar*
3 level tbsp caster sugar	*275 ml double cream*
a pinch of salt	*1 tbsp chopped tarragon*

Beat together the eggs, sugar, salt and vinegar in the top of a double boiler (or in a stainless-steel or china bowl suspended over barely simmering water) until thick and mousselike and the whisk leaves thick trails through the mixture (use an electric hand whisk for the speediest results). Remove from the heat and continue beating until lukewarm. Loosely whip the cream and fold into the sauce, together with the tarragon. Serve cold.

Note: The initial base sauce, i.e., without the cream and tarragon, can be made in advance and stored in the fridge in a sealed container for a week, until needed.

Chicory Salad with Mustard Dressing ✢ serves 4

As a young apprentice in the kitchens of a fine French restaurant in Lancashire, I one day found myself at the mercy of chef Champeau's mischievous nature: he had discovered that I did not like chicory.

Now this is like admitting that you do not like chicken tikka masala to an Englishman . . . The next thing I knew, however, was that I had been invited to lunch with Chef and Mrs Chef, where I was forced to eat five courses, all, neatly and naturally, revolving around the astringent chicory family. For it was that salad's particular bitter notes that puckered up my taste buds and gave chef a good excuse to exercise his bitter style of humour. I must, however, thank him, as I now love the stuff.

Right: **Chicory Salad with Mustard Dressing**

For the dressing:

2 tbsp Dijon mustard

2 tbsp red wine vinegar

4–5 tbsp of warm water

Maldon sea salt

300–450 ml groundnut or other
  flavourless oil

For the salad:

8 medium chicories

1 tbsp chopped parsley

freshly ground black pepper

Put the mustard, vinegar, water and salt in a liquidizer. Switch on and blend. With the motor running, add the oil in a thin stream until homogenized. At this stage, if you think the dressing is too thick, add a little more water; if too thin, add more oil and perhaps a smidgen more mustard. The final consistency should be one of loose salad cream.

This recipe makes much more dressing than you will need for 4 salads, but it is a good stand-by to have in the fridge. Keep in a screw-top jar.

To make the salad, cut off the base of each chicory and separate the leaves. Wash briefly and drain well. Pat dry in tea towels. Place in a large bowl and sprinkle over the parsley and pepper. Add 5–6 tbsp of the dressing and gently mix with your hands until all is well coated. Arrange the leaves onto individual plates, architecturally; or serve directly from the bowl, family style.

Salad of Jersey Royals with Asparagus ‡ serves 4

A seasonal warm vegetable salad that is a marriage made in heaven.

When the first of the Jerseys appear, it is only right that they should be simply boiled in salted water with plenty of fresh mint and eaten with melted butter; on their own, in a hot bowl, and in quantity. Make this salad when you have tired of this. Surely not possible?

450 g selected English asparagus

1 large sprig mint

350 g Jersey Royals, scraped
  scrupulously

For the dressing:
juice of 1 lemon
¼ tsp sugar
75g unsalted butter, the best you can
  afford, cut into small chunks

2 tsp chopped chives
Maldon sea salt
freshly ground white pepper
chervil leaves

Prepare the asparagus by cutting the tips off about 5 cm down (use the stalks for a soup perhaps) and then cut in two on the diagonal. Put a pan of salted water on to boil; simmer the potatoes in another pan of lightly salted water with the mint and keep warm in the water.

Now take a roomy, shallow stainless-steel or enamelled saucepan and squeeze in the lemon juice. Add 6 tbsp of the potato cooking water and the sugar, and simmer this mixture until reduced by half. Using a small whisk over a thread of heat, slowly incorporate the butter a chunk at a time (this is essentially a light butter sauce), until limpid and homogeneous.

Boil the asparagus tips rapidly in the salted water and drain. Similarly drain the warm potatoes and add both to the butter sauce. Turn gently into the sauce, together with the chives, until all are evenly coated. Spoon onto warmed plates, sprinkle with a little salt and pepper and generously scatter the chervil over – it's not just there to look tarty, for once.

Potted *and* Cured Meats

Potted Beef ✣ serves plenty

It is really charming when a reader writes in to say how much they have enjoyed the column. I like it when there is an interactive business going on, and in cases such as these, beneficial to me in more ways than one: I collect a great recipe.

In July 1995, one Glenys K. Pople from Stockport in Cheshire wrote to me extolling the virtues of potted meats. Well, she couldn't have chosen a more enthusiastic recipient if she had tried. Potted meats are one of the most comforting things to eat, nibble at, snack upon or with which to begin a meal – potted anything, if it comes to that.

Shrimps, potted, are one of my most favoured first courses at any time, so too is ham and tongue potted together and served with Cumberland sauce. Salmon mixed with butter, mace and cayenne, and further seasoned up with a little anchovy essence is also good. And then there is the Pople potted beef.

The way the beef was described to me from this good woman is worth the reading in itself. She suggests that it is a handy thing to have around the place at Christmas and goes on to say that when sliced 'makes the most excellent sandwiches ever. We have them every year for tea on Christmas Day.' Or it can be 'served with sauté potatoes and whatever vegetable and/or relish you like. Hot beetroot goes particularly well . . .'

What intrigued me most, however, was the frugal list of ingredients:

shin beef
salt and pepper
water

Here is the recipe, as sent to me.

'Buy 3–4 lbs beef (1.4–1.8 kilos), which must be shin beef from the lower leg of the beast as this recipe will not work with any other cut. It will work with any amount but it's hardly worth doing with less.

Cut off the fat and any horrible bits but leave as much of the inter-connective tissue as possible. This will dissolve in cooking. Cut the beef into cubes that are a little bigger than a quarter of an inch. It takes an age but have patience and a cup of your favourite beverage to keep you going as this step is vital to the finished dish. Put the beef in a saucepan, add water to cover, bring to the boil and skim until the froth is no longer dirty brown or until you are tired of skimming. It looks very unprepossessing at this stage.

Cover and simmer very gently. Add water from time to time if it looks too dry but do not swamp it. You are aiming for the stage (this may take three to four hours) at which the meat "goes to rags" – where each piece of meat will easily separate into individual fibres. Boil hard to drive off any excess water whilst at the same time stirring the mixture vigorously with a fork to break the meat down. At the end the mixture should be moist but not wet. Test it by pushing the meat to one side and tilting the pan. If the liquid runs out, boil for a moment or two longer.

Season with salt and pepper, bearing in mind that you will be serving this cold and it needs more than if you were to be serving it hot.

Pile into (tradition says) an old-fashioned pudding bowl, the sort that you might use for a steamed pudding. Pack down well. Put a saucer on top. Weight down with the family Bible.

Leave to cool for 24 hours on (tradition again) a cold flagged floor, by the end of which it should be set and you can remove the Bible.

The flavour will improve over the next couple of days.

Turn out of the bowl and slice.

Notes:

1. This is plain and honest food that depends on true flavours. You could vary the recipe by adding other seasonings but I have never found them to be an improvement. A dash of soy is just about OK but even Worcestershire Sauce is a distraction. Much better to leave it as it is and if you want more complex flavours, do another recipe.

2. The meat when pressed will only hold together if there was sufficient gelatinous material present in the meat. Being very particular and a bit squeamish, I trim my meat well initially but put the less nasty trimmings in a separate pot to simmer away at the same time and use this "stock" instead of water for topping up.

3. For those who have neither pudding bowls nor family Bible, it works perfectly with any sort of container (rectangular ones will make slicing easier). If necessary get a piece of stiff card, cut it to size, wrap it in cling-film or foil, pop it on top of the meat and weight with a couple of tins. Instead of the cold flagged floor I do the best that I can and refrigerate once it is reasonably cool.

4. As simple as the recipe is it does depend on a certain amount of judgement for its sliceability. If it won't slice neatly, never mind. It will still taste wonderful.'

Thank you, Glenys K. Pople, for your unique recipe.

Bacon du Bedat ✝ makes 4 sandwiches

I first read about this extraordinarily good sandwich in Simon Loftus's terrific book of reminiscences, *A Pike in the Basement – Tales of a Hungry Traveller*. Amongst fifteen or so beguiling recipes peppered throughout the book is this great late-night snack, for when you have the munchies.

The curious – though remarkably delicious – ingredients involve toasted thin-cut white bread, grilled bacon, smoked salmon and mango chutney. It is essential that the bacon should be thin, hot and crisp.

8 slices thin-cut white bread
a little softened butter
4 dsp mango chutney
4 thin slices smoked salmon,
    approximately the shape of
    2 slices of bread
12 small and very thin slices of
    rindless streaky bacon, lightly and
carefully grilled until super-crisp
(Italian smoked pancetta, bought
from a good delicatessen, can be
sliced for you in the shop almost
to the thinness of prosciutto: this
will be perfect)
plenty of freshly ground black or
    cayenne pepper

Toast the bread and thinly spread each slice with the butter, then the chutney. On each slice of toast lay the sheet of smoked salmon, with the extra amount overlapping. Neatly lay the 3 slices of bacon on the part

liquid in a food processor until smooth. Add the minced pork to it, but only process to mix rather than purée the minced meat further. Tip into a roomy bowl.

Trim the chicken livers of any sinew and green stains and quickly fry in the remaining butter until just coloured but very pink within: bouncy to the touch. Tip onto a plate to cool.

Now mix in the ham, *pancetta* or bacon, pork fat and ox tongue with a wooden spoon, together with the garlic and herbs. Beat in the eggs, salt, pepper and nutmeg. Cut the cooled chicken livers into small dice and add these to the mixture too. Melt the gelatine over a low heat with 1 tbsp of water and stir in, along with the cream.

Preheat the oven to 325°F/160°C/gas mark 3.

Line a 1 litre capacity pâté dish with the pork back fat or *pancetta*, leaving a generous over-hang around the rim. Fill with the pâté mixture and give the dish a few sharp taps on a chopping board to settle the filling and disperse air bubbles. Fold the over-hang onto the surface and smooth off with a spatula. Cover with foil, or put on the lid if the dish has one, and place in a deep roasting tin. Fill with hot water to come to at least three-quarters of the way up the outside of the pâté. Bake in the oven for 30 minutes and then turn down the heat to 300°F/150°C/gas mark 2. Cook for a further 35–40 minutes, or until when a skewer is inserted into the middle of the pâté it is hot when touched to the lips; this, by the way, is the best way to test whether pâtés and terrines are cooked.

Remove from the roasting tin and tip away the water. Return the pâté to the empty tin and allow to cool for 10 minutes. Cut a piece of thick cardboard to fit the shape of the pâté's surface and wrap in foil twice. Place on top of the pâté and weight down with two or three tins. Leave like this until completely cold, then store in the fridge.

To serve, run a knife around the edge of the pâté and tip out onto a board. Cut in slices and serve with hot buttered toast and *cornichons*.

Gammon and Spinach ✣ serves 6

After roast chicken cooked with butter, this dish of ham and creamed spinach runs a very close second as one of my favourite things to eat.

The name of the dish also has a nice ring to it; I thought that it would be a good name for a restaurant one day, in fact. But I have always remembered the jolly children's rhyme that you will find at the beginning of this book, and this is possibly the real reason as to why it is titled so.

900 g piece of boneless gammon or
    shoulder
2 carrots, peeled and diced
2 onions, peeled and chopped
2 sticks celery, chopped
2 bay leaves
3–4 sprigs thyme
12 peppercorns
275 ml milk

2 cloves
1 small onion, peeled and chopped
Maldon sea salt
50 g butter
50 g plain flour
75 ml single cream
freshly grated nutmeg
pepper
1.5 kg washed spinach

Put the ham into a large pan and cover with cold water. Bring just to the boil and drain into a colander. Discard the water and rinse the ham under cold running water. Put the ham back into the pan, just cover with cold water and add the vegetables, herbs and peppercorns. Bring up to a simmer and gently cook for about 1½ hours. The meat is ready when it is tender enough to be pierced right through with a skewer. Keep warm in this cooking water.

Heat together the milk, cloves, onion and a little salt. Simmer for a few minutes, cover and allow the flavours to mingle off the heat for about 30 minutes. In another pan, melt the butter and stir in the flour. Make a roux and gently cook the butter and flour together for a minute or two. Strain the milk into the roux and vigorously whisk together until smooth. On the lowest possible heat, set the sauce to cook. You may think that it is very thick, but this is intentional so that it has enough body to hold the chopped spinach in suspension. Do not cover the sauce, stir from time to time with a wooden spoon and cook for about 15 minutes. Meanwhile, briefly blanch the spinach in salted boiling water, drain, refresh in very cold running water, squeeze out with your hands until completely dry and then finely chop it. Add the cream, nutmeg, pepper and spinach to the sauce, mix in thoroughly, check for seasoning and heat through for a few minutes.

Lift the skin from the ham (or not – I quite like it left on) and slice thickly onto a hot platter. Serve the creamed spinach in a handsome bowl and serve separately. Some buttered new potatoes would seem the appropriate carbohydrate here, if you feel the need for it.

Boiled Bacon with Cabbage and Mustard Sauce ⁘ serves 4

One for the colder months. I would almost prefer to eat boiled bacon than gammon, as I really like the fatty strata that run through the belly.

You will have to search out a good butcher for this dish to be good, as supermarkets sadly (and ignorantly) gave up on the idea of properly cured streaky bacon, sold in a piece, years ago now. There is no need to presoak the bacon. Cook a few split peas in the resultant stock to serve with the dish too if you like, or make a lovely soup out of them.

600–700g smoked or unsmoked streaky bacon, in a piece, rind intact
2 large onions, peeled and stuck with 4 cloves each
2 large carrots, peeled and cut into lengths
4 sticks celery, chopped in two
2 leeks, cleaned, trimmed and washed
1 glass dry white wine
bouquet garni

1 medium green cabbage (the best for this is the semi-hard pale green variety), cut into 8 wedges, cores included
3 tbsp chopped flat-leaf parsley

For the mustard sauce:
275ml whipping cream
2 tbsp good quality Dijon mustard
3–4 dashes of Tabasco

Put the bacon in a solid-based pan and just cover with cold water. Bring to the boil, but just before it does so, turn down to a simmer. Skim off all the scum that will have formed and add the vegetables, wine and bouquet garni. Simmer gently for 1 hour. Remove the bacon and keep warm (in a steamer would be ideal). Discard the vegetables and bouquet garni. Simmer the cabbage in the remaining water until good and tender. Drain well, reserving the broth, and cut the cores away. Lay out onto a handsome warmed platter, cover with foil and keep warm in a low oven.

Remove a couple of ladles of the cooking broth to a small pan (keep the remaining broth for that split-pea soup I mentioned, or freeze it for another time) and reduce a little until well flavoured; watch out for excess salt, however. When the taste has intensified, add the parsley. Slice the bacon into thickish pieces and lay over the cabbage (watch out for more water which may have seeped out of the cabbage; if so drain it off). Spoon over some of the parsley liquid.

To make the mustard sauce, heat the cream in a small saucepan and whisk in the mustard and Tabasco. Simmer for about 5 minutes until custardy-thick and unctuous. A few small capers stirred in at the last minute are a nice idea, and mashed potatoes are de rigueur, I feel.

Fish *and* Shellfish

Anguille au Vert   ⁙   serves 3–4

Skinning a freshly killed eel is not in any way as difficult or as worrisome as you think. Just behind the head, make a circular cut through the skin. Now, with a pair of pliers and holding onto the head with a damp tea towel or dishcloth, pull away the skin sharply with some determination and fortitude: it will peel away from the flesh as one long inverted bicycle inner tube. Trust me.

Having sifted through several good recipes for *Anguille au Vert*, I have come up with a combination of herbs and greenery that suits my taste just fine. Although the dish may be served hot or cold, I prefer the latter. It would be perfect for a summer lunch out of doors eaten with hot new potatoes, the contrast of cold and hot being particularly delicious.

50g butter
75g watercress leaves, chopped
75g sorrel leaves, chopped
4 sprigs mint, leaves only, chopped
12–15 sprigs flat-leaf parsley, leaves only, chopped
8 sprigs tarragon, leaves only, chopped
1 tbsp chopped lovage leaves if you can find some, or celery leaves
1 small bunch spring onions, trimmed and finely chopped

1 x 450g piece of eel, gutted and skinned, cut into 5cm lengths (the ideal width of the eel should be about 4cm)
Maldon sea salt and freshly ground black pepper
200ml dry white wine
3 large egg yolks
2 tbsp double cream
a squeeze of lemon juice

Melt the butter in a deepish shallow pan that has a lid, and put in all the greenery and herbs and the spring onions. Allow to stew gently for a few minutes and then put in the eel on top. Season and pour over the wine. Bring up to a very, very gentle simmer and cover. Cook for 15 minutes. Lift out the eel and put into a (preferably) deep white dish. Beat the egg yolks and cream together, then incorporate into the mulchy liquor, stirring as you go. Cook very gently over a thread of heat until the sauce starts to thicken, but watch that you don't scramble the egg. Check for seasoning, add the lemon juice and pour over the eel. Put in the fridge to chill for at least 3 hours, covered with clingfilm.

Lobster Courchamps, or 'A Sauce for Boiled Lobster' ✣

makes enough sauce to spoon generously over 2 hot, split lobsters

This sensationally good recipe comes from *An Omelette and a Glass of Wine*, by Elizabeth David. In her book, Mrs David calls the dish Lobster Courchamps. She named it after the Comte de Courchamps (who is attributed to have written the first of three books, published 1839, where Mrs David found this recipe), as the sauce was not named. I like the last sentence in the introduction to the recipe: 'Highly imaginative as they were, all three gentlemen (authors of those three books) called it Sauce for Boiled Lobster.'

coral of two lobsters (optional)
2 small shallots, peeled and finely
    chopped
1 tsp chopped tarragon leaves
2 tbsp chopped parsley
Maldon sea salt and freshly ground
    black pepper
1 level tsp Dijon mustard
24–30 drops soy sauce

approx. 6 tbsp fruity, extra-virgin
    olive oil
juice of 1 small lemon
1 tsp anisette de Bordeaux *(Pernod*
    can just *– and I mean* just *– be*
    used as an alternative, but buy
    one bottle of the anisette and,
    as Mrs David points out, it will
    last for some time)

In a small bowl mash up the coral, if using, with the shallots, tarragon and parsley; otherwise just mix the shallots and herbs together. Add seasonings, mustard and soy sauce. Whisk all together thoroughly and then add the oil in a thin stream as if making a vinaigrette. Stir in the lemon juice and anisette.

Chilled Lobster Gazpacho ‡ serves 4

This soup could be made with prawns, or perhaps crabmeat. However, the depth of sweet lobster flavour in the soup, due to the infusion of shells, would be sorely missed. It is loosely based upon a dish that I ate for lunch at a remarkable restaurant called El Bulli, near Cadaques, in northern Spain, about three years ago. The restaurant, situated upon a small and remote beach and reached only by a seven-kilometre rough road, has recently had bestowed upon it three stars by the Michelin guide. Let's hope this does not spoil its special charm. Lunch does not really get going until about 3.30 p.m.

Part 1:
2 x 500g live hen lobsters
2 tbsp tarragon vinegar
4 tbsp olive oil
Maldon sea salt and freshly ground
   black pepper

Part 2:
the shells of the lobsters
4–5 slices of fresh ginger
1 clove of garlic, crushed
2 tbsp cognac
570ml tomato passata (fresh pure
   pasteurized tomato pulp, sieved,
   sold in cartons)
300ml water
3 sprigs tarragon, roughly
   chopped

Part 3:
½ green pepper, chopped
½ red pepper, chopped
½ cucumber, peeled and chopped
1 small red onion, peeled and chopped
2 tbsp tarragon vinegar
Maldon sea salt
a few shakes Tabasco
150ml whipping cream

For the garnish:
1 tbsp each finely chopped red and
   green peppers, red onion, cucumber
   and tomato flesh
very thin croutons cut from a small
   baguette, smeared with olive oil,
   crushed garlic and parsley, then
   baked in a moderate oven until
   crisp and golden
a drizzle of extra-virgin olive oil
a little chopped tarragon

Ask your fishmonger to kill the lobsters and cut them in half, or do it yourself if you feel brave enough. Remove the stomach sac, which lies in the head, and also the central grey digestive tract. Crack the claws with the back of a heavy knife.

Put each lobster on a deep plate and spoon over the vinegar and olive oil. Season. Cook separately, in two batches, in a steamer for 15 minutes. Remove and cool slightly. Lift the flesh from the carapace and put onto a plate to cool. Tip the shells and every scrap of their juices into a pan. Add the rest of the ingredients in part 2. Bring to a simmer, and cook gently for 45 minutes. Strain into a deep bowl through a colander and leave to drip for 10 minutes or so. Add all the ingredients of part 3 apart from the cream. Liquidize in batches until very smooth and pass through a sieve into yet another bowl. Stir in the cream, check for seasoning and chill for at least 3 hours. Pour into chilled shallow soup plates, add the lobster flesh cut into chunks and sprinkle over the diced vegetable garnish. Arrange the croutons around the edge of the plates, drizzle with a little olive oil and scatter with the tarragon.

Hake with Salsa Verde ‡ serves 4

During another visit to Spain a couple of years ago, Madrid to be more precise, and in and around Toledo to be exact, I ate, for the first time, *merluza con salsa verde*. Now this has nothing to do with the Italian edition of 'green sauce'; it is in fact more akin to English parsley sauce than that emulsion of olive oil, green herbs, capers and anchovies.

The nice people we had lunch with, and where I ate my *merluza* (hake, don't you know, and best beloved fish of the Spanish), are local curers of Serrano ham. As the restaurant where they entertained us was well known to them, I asked if it would be possible to have the famous hake in green sauce. I had quickly sussed that it was not about to be included in the verbal menu that was being swiftly delivered – nay gabbled, and what with my understanding of Spanish not being any good, I thought I should listen

Right: **Hake with Salsa Verde**

keenly for the word '*merlutha*' (the 'z' I at least did know is pronounced 'th', as in 'think I should learn thomè Thpanish').

As it happened, they were only too delighted to serve me the second most famous Spanish dish after Paella, and a cracker it was too. I had duly read over the years what a wonderful thing this dish of green hake could be, but, as is the way of things regional and recipe-bound, the version on this occasion was not like any I had previously put into the gastronomic-world memory bank.

First of all, two short lengths of tinned white Spanish asparagus were perched atop the fish, which in turn sat in a pale limpid sauce the colour of strained milky porridge, almost jelled in consistency, yet hot. Just discernible flecks of dull green parsley floated about a bit, and the only true key note was the deep brown, well-used, terracotta dish that it was served in. There were no clams, peas or mussels, as I had read about before, nor was the more prosaic onion included. It was simply hake, slightly browned garlic, perhaps a smidgen of white wine, olive oil, the restrained parsley and the juice from the fish as it cooked.

The addition of the tinned asparagus was actually delicious, and I reckon some of the juice from the tin might have been included too. Have you ever had tinned Spanish asparagus, by the way? It is highly thought of in the Iberian peninsula, and comes in deep rectangular tins; both container and contents are very handsome to behold and the asparagus tastes really good.

4–6 tbsp olive oil
4 cloves garlic, peeled and
   sliced
Maldon sea salt and freshly ground
   black pepper
1 tbsp plain flour

4 thick hake fillets, around 150–200g
   each, skinned and any tiny bones
   removed with tweezers; or failing
   hake, cod
1 small glass dry white wine
3 tbsp chopped flat-leaf parsley

Heat the oil in a terracotta dish (or shallow cast-iron pot or deep frying pan) and throw in the garlic. Allow to become pale golden over a low heat, and then lift out of the pot onto a plate. Turn up the heat slightly, season and lightly flour the fish fillets and lay in the garlic-flavoured oil.

Gammon and Spinach

Fry gently until a little coloured on each side and add the wine. Lift and tilt the dish so that the wine runs around and under the fish. Set to simmer for a few minutes, add the garlic back to the dish and sprinkle over the parsley. Put a tight-fitting lid on the pot, or foil. After 30 seconds, switch off the heat and leave to rest and finish cooking for 10 minutes.

Lift off the lid or foil and check that the fish is cooked. Bring back to a simmer and shake the pan around a bit, so that the parsley disperses through the sauce (you may use a wildly inauthentic spoon here – I did), and the olive oil emulsifies into the juices. Practice makes perfect, I'm afraid. And with that motto in mind, it makes me feel a bit better to admit that I actually put the sauce into the liquidizer for a quick blast.

Note: If you don't think you have enough liquid, add a splash of water.

Twiddled Prawns   serves 4

The damn silly name for these quite delicious prawns is the affectionate title for any dish cooked by my parents that just came about by fiddling (or twiddling) about in the kitchen.

The fenugreek should preferably be in its dried *herb* form and is sold under the name *methi* (as in *aloo methi*, potatoes cooked with fenugreek, often seen amongst the vegetable dishes in many a local tandoori house). This is not easily available, but can be readily found in Indian stores in your vicinity. Alternatively, and if you live in far-flung regions, ask your nearest Indian restaurant where they get theirs from and they might be able to furnish you with the address of a wholesaler. It keeps quite well if kept in a tightly sealed container or plastic bag. Otherwise, buy ground fenugreek seeds as a spice, which can be found on most supermarket spice racks. This ivory coloured powder does not give quite the same flavour as the herb, but has a similar odour; it makes up the bulk of most commercially produced curry powders and it is in fact the ground fenugreek seed that you smell most here. If you have to use the spice, add a little freshly chopped coriander leaf to the sauce at the end. For the clarified butter, see Potato Pancakes with Smoked Eel, Bacon and Horseradish, page 64.

4 medium thick slices of bread from a
    non-sliced small white loaf, crusts
    removed
clarified butter
25g butter
1 medium onion, peeled and finely
    chopped
1 small clove garlic, finely chopped
2 healthy pinches of dried fenugreek
    herb, or 1 level tsp ground
    fenugreek plus chopped coriander
    leaves

2 small tomatoes, skinned, deseeded
    and finely chopped
1 tsp plain flour
75ml milk
75ml double cream
a squeeze of lemon juice
225–275g prawns (defrosted/shelled
    weight); frozen will be OK, fresh
    are naturally better

Fry the bread in the clarified butter until golden brown on each side, drain on kitchen paper and keep warm in a low oven.

Melt the butter and fry the onion and garlic until softened and pale golden. Add the fenugreek and allow to cook for a minute or two. Stir in the tomatoes and cook out their moisture. Add the flour, stir in till well blended and pour in the milk. Cook as for a basic white sauce and add the cream. Allow to simmer gently until thickened to a creamy consistency. Add the prawns, heat through, add the coriander if using, and spoon over the fried bread. Serve immediately.

Warm Haricot Bean Salad with Seafood   ✣   serves 4

Almost any combination of seafood and shellfish may be used in this conglomeration; it's really up to you and what you like to eat. Put some lobster in if you please, or scallops, or little brown shrimps, it doesn't matter. It should be based simply on what is best the day the dish is prepared.

200g dried white haricot, cannellini or
    flageolet beans

1 onion stuck with 4 cloves
2 bay leaves

Left: **Twiddled Prawns**

2 carrots, peeled

3 celery ribs, washed and cut in half

20 medium clams

4 dozen fresh mussels, cleaned and
    debearded

½ bottle dry white wine

700g cooked, shell-on frozen prawns
    (the size to buy will give you
    25–30 prawns per 500g),
    defrosted and shelled – keep
    the shells

8 small to medium prepared squid
    tubes (available from supermarkets)

6 tbsp olive oil

2 tbsp red wine vinegar

Maldon sea salt and cayenne
    pepper

2 shallots or 4 spring onions, finely
    sliced

4 large tomatoes, peeled, deseeded and
    chopped into dice

3 tbsp chopped flat-leaf parsley

juice of ½ a lemon

Put the beans in a pot and cover with several inches of cold water. Leave to soak overnight. The next day, wash the beans thoroughly, put into a pan and cover with fresh water. Bring to the boil and then drain and rinse with cold water (this helps get rid of initial excess scum and – I am told – also helps reduce incessant wind). Return to a clean pan, together with the cloved onion, bay leaves, carrots and celery. Do not add salt, as this can cause the skins of the beans to toughen. Simmer gently until tender – about 1 hour or so. Some scum will form whilst this is going on, so skim the surface occasionally. Now add a little salt and keep the beans warm in the cooking liquor.

Put the clams and mussels in a solid-bottomed pot and pour over the wine. Bring to a boil, shaking the contents until the clams and mussels are open. Lift out with a slotted spoon and set aside, discarding any that are still closed. Add the prawn shells to the cooking liquor and simmer for 15 minutes. Strain through a very fine sieve into another pan and reduce to a few tablespoonfuls. Pour into a small bowl (this will be the bowl in which the dressing will be made).

Grill or fry the squid for a minute or two on each side; both cooking surfaces should be very hot and smeared with a little olive oil. Season, slice into rings and put into a bowl with the prawns. Shell the clams and mussels and mix with the squid and prawns. Make the dressing by combining the vinegar, seasoning (watch the amount of salt, due to the saline content of the reduced mussel/clam juice), remaining olive oil and the shellfish liquor and pour over the shellfish meat. Add the shallots or spring onions, garlic, tomatoes and parsley. Mix well.

Finally (whew!) drain the warm beans (discarding vegetables) and mix with the shellfish. Tip into a suitable shallow serving dish and squeeze over the lemon juice.

Matelote d'Anguille ‡ serves 3–4

I first ate a *matelote* at the legendary Chez Allard on the Left Bank in Paris, nearly twenty years ago now. It was a revelation and remembered as being particularly delicious washed down with a *pichet* of chilled Chiroubles. Once again, I have worked the dish around to suit my own style; the initial flavouring and cooking of the wine is a method I use for all winey stews (*coq au vin*, *bœuf Bourguignonne*, etc.), as it removes excess alcohol, which gives the sauce a softer note.

450g eel, gutted and skinned, cut into 5cm lengths (the ideal width of the eel should be about 4 cm)

2 tbsp cognac

1 tbsp red wine vinegar

For the wine reduction:

slightly more than ½ bottle full-bodied fruity red wine

1 tsp redcurrant jelly

1 small carrot, peeled and chopped

1 small onion, peeled and chopped

1 celery rib, chopped

3 cloves garlic, peeled and bruised with the back of a knife

2 sprigs thyme

1 bay leaf

To finish:

50g butter

75g thinly sliced streaky bacon or pancetta, cut into slivers

12–15 button onions, peeled (place in a bowl of hot water first; they are then easier to peel)

12–15 tiny button mushrooms

2 cloves garlic, peeled and chopped

Maldon sea salt and freshly ground black pepper

1 tsp plain flour

juice of ½ a small lemon

1 tbsp chopped parsley

juice of ½ a small lemon

1 tbsp chopped parsley

Place the eel in a dish with the cognac and vinegar and leave to marinate for 6 hours or overnight.

Put the wine reduction ingredients in a non-reactive (stainless-steel or enamelled) pan and bring to the boil. Ignite the wine with a match and allow the flames to subside. Turn down to a simmer and cook gently for about 30 minutes until reduced by almost half. Strain into a bowl through a fine sieve and reserve.

Melt 25g of the butter in a wide deepish pan and fry the bacon or *pancetta* until coloured. Remove, set aside and add the onions and mushrooms. Cook until golden and just tender, stir in the garlic and reintroduce the bacon or *pancetta*. Pour over the flavoured wine, slip in the eel together with its marinade and season. Allow to simmer very gently for 20 minutes or so. Lift out the solids, put into a warmed dish and keep hot, covered, in a low oven. Mix the remaining butter and the flour to a paste, and incorporate into the sauce, with the aid of a whisk, until smooth. Simmer for 10 minutes to cook out the flour and then stir in the lemon juice. Pour over the eel and sprinkle with the parsley. Serve very hot, with either boiled potatoes or pieces of fried bread or both.

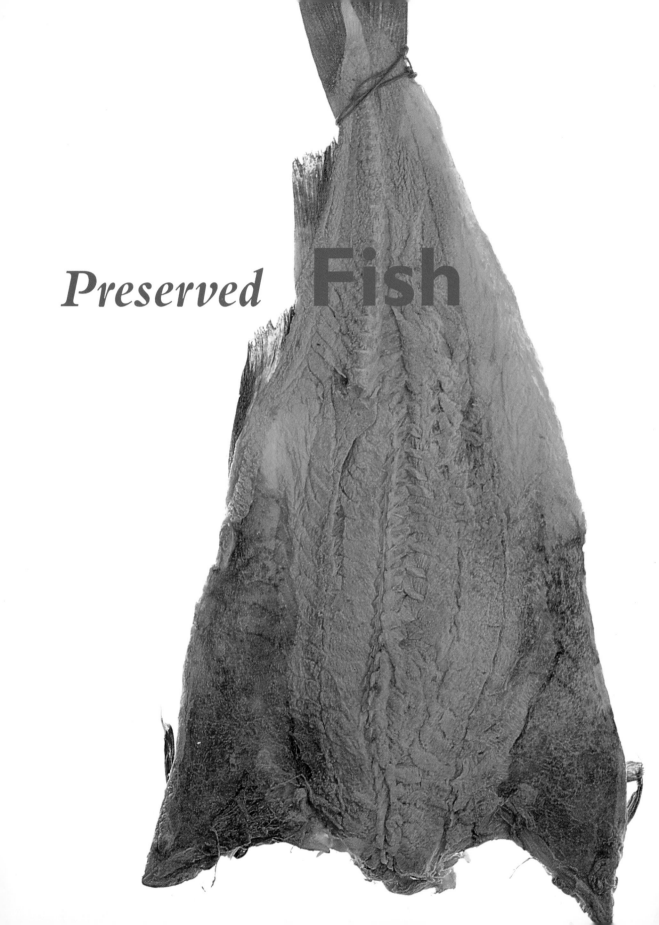

Preserved **Fish**

Potato Pancakes with Smoked Eel, Bacon and Horseradish ‡ serves 4

This recipe is a sublime combination of textures and flavours. The warm and soft pancakes, the crisp salty bacon, the oiliness of the smoked fish and the cool, 'hot' sauce, all contrast each with each other in a most effective manner.

The potato pancakes are based upon the famous 'Crêpes Parmentier' that I first ate at the legendary restaurant Georges Blanc, in Vonnas, Burgundy. Here they are served alongside the luxuriously rich 'Poulet à la crème grand-mère Blanc' or filled with slivers of smoked salmon and napped with a lemon cream sauce. Both dishes are alone worth the journey to Vonnas.

For the pancake batter:
500g potatoes, peeled and cut into
large chunks
50 ml milk
2½ tbsp plain flour
3 eggs
4 egg whites
2½ tbsp double cream
Maldon sea salt and freshly ground
*   black pepper*
a little clarified butter (melt some
*   butter, allow to settle, skim off froth*
*   and pour off clear butter, leaving*

the milky residue behind. Keeps
well in the fridge, so melt a
whole packet)
225g smoked eel fillets
8 very thin rashers of rindless, smoked
*   streaky bacon, grilled until crisp*

For the horseradish:
1 piece of fresh horseradish root, about
*   10 cm long, peeled*
150 ml double cream
a squeeze of lemon juice
Maldon sea salt

Steam the potatoes until tender. Whilst still hot, put through a *mouli-légumes* or a potato masher on the finest setting. Put into a mixing bowl and beat in the milk, flour, eggs, egg whites, cream and seasoning.

Heat a little of the clarified butter in a non-stick pan or on a flat griddle. Take 1 tbsp of batter and pour onto the surface of the pan. Keep the heat moderate to high; you need a slight sizzle and a light browning at the edges of the pancake after about 2 minutes. The time to turn over is when tiny bubbles appear on the uncooked surface. Take a palette knife and quickly flip them over. The cooked surface should be mottled with pale brown blisters and have a thin golden ring around the edge. Finish cooking for a further minute or so; the texture should be slightly springy. As you cook the pancakes, keep them in a very low oven on a large plate, uncovered.

Finely grate the horseradish into a bowl. Mix in the cream, lemon juice and salt and stir until thick: this does not take long.

Assembling the pancakes is entirely a matter for you. I would suggest 3 pancakes per serving, with the eel and bacon being cut and divided to allow for four servings. The assembly can be attractive stacked up in a little tower, with the eel and bacon being secured in place by dabs of the creamed horseradish. Or you can lay the pancakes out flat on a plate, each being topped with small pieces of eel and bacon, then topped with a small spoonful of horseradish and sprinkled with chives. And a final idea might also be to serve them as canapés, but you will have to make very small pancakes here. Also the eel and bacon will have to be cut into tiny slivers. Time-consuming work, but guests and friends will applaud and think you are glamorous and wonderful.

Salt Cod Hash ✠ serves 2

Great slabs of salt cod fill small shop windows in the back streets of Oporto. Its odour – and it does possess a particularly niffy one – drifted down the street. 'I think there is one just around the corner,' I muttered, sniffing, to my friend Lindsey when we were there once, on a trip to the port cellars of Messrs Sandeman.

The vendor cut through the stinky-salty, board-stiff planks of it with a well-honed serrated knife of bandsaw calibre. But it don't come cheap, and there are varying grades from the super-duper whole fish and prime central cuts down to the stringy and fibrous side and tail pieces, all priced accordingly.

To find good salt cod in the UK is not that easy, so I would urge you to bring some home from foreign holidays (Spain, northern Italy,

southern France and all over Portugal are prime areas to pick up salt cod).
Otherwise, search out Portuguese or Spanish shops in London and other
major cities. The two shops Garcia, in London's Portobello Road, or
Lisboa, in nearby Golborne Road (both London W10), are where I get my
particular fix.

1 tbsp olive oil
75g streaky bacon (pancetta is good),
     cut into slivers
1 medium potato, peeled, cut into dice,
     boiled till tender and well drained
175g salt cod

1 large clove garlic, peeled and chopped
3 spring onions, finely chopped
2 hard-boiled eggs, shelled and grated
1 tbsp chopped parsley
1–2 tbsp red wine vinegar
freshly ground black pepper

Take a roomy (preferably non-stick) frying pan and pour in the olive oil.
Fry the bacon in it until crisp and then add the potato dice. Continue
cooking until the potatoes have also browned and stir in the cod, garlic,
spring onions and eggs. Stir-fry briskly for 3–4 minutes until all is well
coloured and then finally mix in the parsley and vinegar. Tip onto a
warmed serving dish and grind over the pepper. Eat at once.

Brandade de Morue   ✢   serves 4

Some recipes for brandade call for a small amount of puréed potato, added
for bulk and to retain a firmer texture. But I prefer to do without. If made
carefully and slowly, the flesh of the cod, once having been broken down
in a food processor, should absorb all the oil and milk, as when making
mayonnaise. Traditionally, brandade – and also the Provençal aïoli – is made
in a pestle and mortar, vigorously, and usually by Provençal women, with
strong arms. So if that is how you see yourself, then by all means make it
in this time-honoured fashion.

   Note: The addition of parsley at the end is a matter for you. The
Venetian version of the French brandade is called baccalà mantecato and
always includes a lot of chopped parsley. I like this.

*500g dried salt cod, soaked in several
    changes of cold water, for 24 hours
3 cloves garlic, peeled and crushed to a
    paste with a little salt
75 ml warm milk*

*150–200 ml fruity olive oil, warmed
    until tepid
juice of 1 small lemon
1 tbsp chopped flat-leaf parsley
freshly ground black pepper*

Cover the cod with cold water in a pan and simmer ever so gently for about 15 minutes. Drain, carefully remove any bones and skin, flake the flesh and put back into the (wiped out) pan. Add the milk and 75 ml of the oil. Warm through together for a few moments so that the fish absorbs most of the oil and milk. Tip into the bowl of a food processor with the garlic. Pulverize for a few seconds, but do not overwork. Now, with the motor running, start to add the oil in a thin stream, stopping from time to time and scraping down the sides with a spatula. When the *baccalà* looks glossy and homogeneous, it is ready (if you have not used all the oil, don't worry, it can still be used in something else). Add the lemon juice, parsley and pepper and mix in. Serve warm with grilled polenta, as is the way in Venice, or olive oil brushed slices of grilled country bread, or fried *croûtes*, as they might in Nîmes.

Baked Salt Cod and Potatoes with Cream and Garlic ✣ for 4 hefty servings

If you like to eat the classic French *gratin Dauphinois* – that gorgeous creamy bubbling mass of potatoes, garlic and cream – then you should like this dish very much indeed. The pungent cod adds a further dimension and turns the dish into a complete meal in itself, eaten, perhaps, with a crisp green salad that has been simply dressed with excellent olive oil and lemon juice. I am tentative to admit it, but am rather partial to a small plateful of any leftover cold bits of this the morning after, to aid curing a particularly vile hangover.

550g dried salt cod, soaked in several changes of cold water for 24 hours
a little butter
1kg medium potatoes, peeled
275 ml double cream
275 ml whipping cream
5 large cloves garlic, peeled and finely chopped
Maldon sea salt and freshly ground black pepper
1 small bunch flat-leaf parsley, leaves only, finely chopped

Preheat the oven to 375°F/190°C/gas mark 5.

Put the cod in a large pan and cover with cold water. Slowly bring up to *just* simmering (trembling water) and poach very gently for about 5 minutes. Carefully lift out onto a plate with a slotted spoon and leave to cool slightly. Remove all the flesh from the bones and put onto a plate. Note: it is important for the fish to be still warm when removing the bones, as once cold it is difficult to separate the two due to the high degree of gelatine, and it all sticks together.

Lightly butter a generous sized oval or round ovenproof dish. Slice the potatoes thinly (£1 coin thickness). Mix the two creams together and whisk in the garlic. Cover the base of the dish with a single layer of potatoes and then strew with some of the salt cod. Lightly season with salt and pepper and pour about a quarter of the garlic-infused cream over. Strew with some of the parsley and then repeat this process until all the ingredients are exhausted, ending with a layer of potatoes. With the flat of your hand, gently press the layers allowing the cream to rise and run over the top layer of potatoes. This will give the surface of the dish a sumptuous golden crust once the dish is cooked. Put into the oven for 20 minutes and then turn the temperature down to 300°F/150°C/gas mark 2 and cook for a further 30–40 minutes. Test with a skewer to see that the potatoes are cooked through, remove from the oven and allow to cool for 10 minutes before serving. Dishes such as these are not so good eaten piping hot. Eat with a crisp green salad if you must, or nothing at all, but it is very, very rich.

Smoked Haddock Pancakes with Curry Cream Sauce ‡ serves 4

I love this sort of thing; creamy and soft with the right level of spice to add more savour. It immediately makes me feel greedy just thinking about it . . . Imagine wrapped-up soggy kedgeree and you will have just about the right idea.

For the pancake batter:
50g plain flour
a pinch of salt
1 egg
150ml milk
25g butter, melted
a little more melted butter for greasing the frying pan

For the haddock:
500g un-dyed smoked haddock fillets, bones removed
700 ml milk
2 bay leaves
25g butter
6 spring onions, trimmed and finely chopped
1 tsp plain flour
3 hard-boiled eggs, shelled and chopped

1 tbsp chopped coriander
Maldon sea salt and freshly ground black pepper

For the curry cream sauce:
1 small onion, peeled and finely chopped
25g butter
1 tbsp curry powder
1 tsp tomato purée
1 level tbsp plain flour
275ml milk from cooking the smoked haddock
1 dsp mango chutney
75ml cream
juice of ½ a lemon
Maldon sea salt and freshly ground black pepper
a handful of coriander leaves (optional)

First make the pancake batter by simply putting all the ingredients in a liquidizer and blending well. Pour through a sieve into a jug and allow to stand for at least 30 minutes. Take a 15 cm frying pan, melt a small amount of butter and allow it to become hot and sizzling. Pour in enough batter to thinly cover the base of the pan. The first pancake is often a bit of a mess; if so chuck it out and then start afresh. Make 8 pancakes and put on one side.

Gammon and Spinach

70

Cut the haddock into manageable pieces that will fit snugly into a pan, and pour over the milk. Add the bay leaves and poach ever so gently for about 5 minutes. Leave in the milk to cool to lukewarm. Now lift out the fish, put onto a plate and lift off the skin. Flake the flesh into a bowl and put on one side, and reserve the milk.

Melt the butter in a small pan, fry the spring onions until soft and add the flour. Cook very gently for a couple of minutes and then add 150 ml of the cooking milk to form an onion sauce. Mix into the flaked fish along with the eggs and coriander. Check the seasoning. Divide between the 8 pancakes and neatly roll up, tucking in the ends as you go. Place in a lightly buttered ovenproof dish and set on one side.

Preheat the oven to 350°F/180°C/gas mark 4.

To make the curry cream sauce, first fry the onion in the butter until pale golden. Add the curry powder and allow to cook gently for 3–4 minutes, mix in the tomato purée and then add the flour. Stir well and pour in the 275 ml of poaching milk. Bring up to a simmer, stirring constantly, and add the mango chutney. Cook on a low light for about 15 minutes. Strain through a fine sieve into a clean pan and add the cream. Bring back up to a simmer and add the lemon juice. Check the seasoning and then pour over the pancakes. Bake in the preheated oven for 25 minutes until bubbling and lightly burnished. Sprinkle with leaves of coriander if desired.

Smoked Cod's Roe with *Piperade* ‡

serves 4

Piperade is quite possibly the Basque region's most famous dish. Scrambled egg with bits in would not be an entirely inaccurate description: chopped pimiento, bacon or Bayonne ham, garlic, onions, tomato and sometimes a little chilli pepper. You may also wish to serve this dish as simply a slab of cod's roe with the *piperade* alongside and the buttered toast served separately (see the photograph overleaf).

4 thick slices buttered toast

100g fresh smoked cod's roe, skinned,
   at room temperature

2 thin rashers rindless streaky bacon,
   finely chopped

1 dsp olive oil

1 small clove garlic, finely chopped

3 spring onions, trimmed and finely
   chopped

2 tomatoes, skinned, deseeded and
   finely chopped

½ roasted pimiento, skinned and
   chopped (Spanish ones in jars
   would be perfect here)

6 eggs, beaten

½ tbsp chopped parsley

Maldon sea salt

cayenne pepper

Thickly spread the buttered toast with the cod's roe (as you might with fish paste!) and keep warm in a very low oven.

Fry the bacon in the oil until golden. Add the garlic, spring onions, and tomatoes and cook until most of their moisture has been driven off. Add the pimiento, eggs and parsley and scramble in the usual way. Season with a little salt to taste, remembering that the roe is already salty.

Remove the cod's roe toasts to four plates and pile the *piperade* on top. Sprinkle with a little cayenne and serve without delay.

Filets d'Harengs, Pommes à l'Huile ⚓ serves 4–6

You can find these herrings in 200g packets in specialist fishmongers (look for the words *saur* and *doux* on the packet, also *fumés au feu de bois*), or stock up with some the next time you take a trip to Boulogne-sur-Mer, just across the Channel. They have a fairly long life anyway, but can also be successfully frozen. Also, once submerged in oil, they will keep in the fridge for several weeks, improving and softening as they mature.

2 x 200g packets filets d'harengs

150ml sunflower oil

150ml light olive oil

2 medium carrots, peeled and very
   thinly sliced

2 small onions, peeled and very thinly
   sliced

1 small bulb fennel, trimmed and
   thinly sliced

4–5 sprigs thyme

Left: Smoked Cod's Roe with *Piperade*

4 fresh bay leaves (if possible)	*½ tsp dried chilli flakes*
1 tsp crushed peppercorns	*(optional)*

Cut the herring fillets (there are no bones) into 5cm pieces and put onto a plate. Mix together the oils in a measuring jug. Take a roomy preserving jar (traditional vessel) or lidded plastic box and pour in a layer of the oil. Scatter in some of the vegetables, herbs and spices and add a layer of herring. Keep doing this until all the ingredients are exhausted. However, do make sure that the herrings are covered in oil. Seal the container and allow to macerate for at least one week in a cool dark place. After this time, if you have not used them, store in the fridge.

To serve, boil or steam 5–6 medium waxy-fleshed potatoes in their skins. Once cool enough to handle, but still fairly hot, peel and thickly slice onto warm plates. Lay over several pieces of herring and the vegetables and then spoon over some of the oil so that it soaks into the potatoes. Sprinkle with a little chopped parsley. I like to add a few drops of red wine vinegar to each serving for a touch of acidity, but this is not established behaviour.

Marinated Kipper Fillets ⚜ serves 4

Remember this one? It was a favourite dinner party stand-by about twenty years ago. My mother used to swear by it and grandly suggested that it was every bit as good as smoked salmon. Well, I'm not so sure about that, but it was actually a smashing little first course in its own right. In its own quaint English way, it is not dissimilar to the previous Froggy herring recipe.

8 kipper fillets	*½ tbsp black peppercorns, coarsely*
2 lemons, one squeezed, the other	*crushed*
thinly sliced	*4–5 sprigs thyme*
2 medium onions, peeled and thinly	*a few sprigs of flat-leaf parsley*
sliced	*8 tbsp olive oil*

There is no need to skin the kipper fillets. Take each one, slice at an angle – rather like thick slices of smoked salmon – and put into a deep oval dish. Squeeze over the lemon juice, and distribute the lemon slices. Strew the onions over and scatter with the peppercorns. Then tuck in the thyme and parsley sprigs. Carefully spoon over the olive oil, cover with clingfilm and put into the fridge for 24 hours. Remove to room temperature 1 hour before serving and eat with brown bread and butter. For a light lunch or supper dish, serve up with a bowl of hot buttered new potatoes.

Potted Salmon   serves 6

This is made in a very similar way to potted shrimps, but here we are dealing with raw fish so there is actual cooking going on rather than just heating through. Tarragon or chervil could be used instead of dill and using coarsely crushed black peppercorns may be a more conservative alternative to the green ones.

Contrary to my normal feelings concerning farmed and wild salmon, on this occasion it is just about OK to use the farmed variety here. However, the end result using wild fish will still turn out to be an infinitely better dish, but naturally more costly. Try and bargain with the fishmonger to furnish you with a tail piece; ideal for this dish, which I am sure he will be happy to fillet and skin for you. The total weight here, including skin and bone and to end up with 350g of flesh, should be around 450g.

Other fish that can be potted successfully are very fresh mackerel and kipper fillets. Shellfish such as crab and lobster can be sumptuous when treated in this simple manner and I once had some success with very fresh small prawns, but I had to shell these myself – an arduous task to be sure, but the result was memorable.

1 large juicy lemon
350g salmon flesh, cut into 2.5 cm
   chunks

175g best quality unsalted
   butter
Maldon sea salt

*1 dsp green peppercorns
     (sold in tins packed in brine),
     slightly crushed*

*1 tsp Pernod (optional)
1 tbsp chopped dill and a few sprigs
     for decoration*

First of all, take the lemon and carefully remove the skin and pith with a small sharp knife. To do this, cut off the top and bottom of the lemon and stand it on its end. Slice down in a curving motion as near to the flesh as possible, continuing around the fruit until you end up with a little denuded barrel. Now, with the lemon held on its side in the palm of your hand, start cutting out segments slicing between each membrane – which are quite clearly defined (do this over a bowl so as to catch the juices as well as somewhere to drop the segments as you go). Pick out the segments and chop into dice. Return to the bowl to add to the salmon later. This useful chore, by the way, is also the very best way to prepare grapefruits and oranges for the breakfast table.

Now, melt 100g of the butter in a wide shallow pan and heat until hot but not frothing. Turn the pieces of fish through this, over a very low light, with a wooden spoon. Try not to break up the fish too much, although some falling apart will be inevitable; the trick here is to try and keep the middle part of each chunk a sort of medium-rare, as the fish will carry on cooking in its own heat once removed from the source.

So, off the heat, now add a generous sprinkling of salt (a rich fish once cold, such as salmon, needs ample seasoning), the peppercorns, Pernod if using, the chopped lemon flesh and juice and finally the dill. Pack into ramekins in the same manner as potted shrimps and chill in the fridge. Melt the remaining butter and spoon over the potted salmon to seal, dropping a few sprigs of dill to set into the melted butter as you go. Serve in exactly the same way as you would shrimps. It is good to eat this within 24 hours of making, purely for cosmetic reasons, as the acidity of the lemon can cause the dill to discolour if kept much longer. However, it will taste perfectly good for up to 4 days.

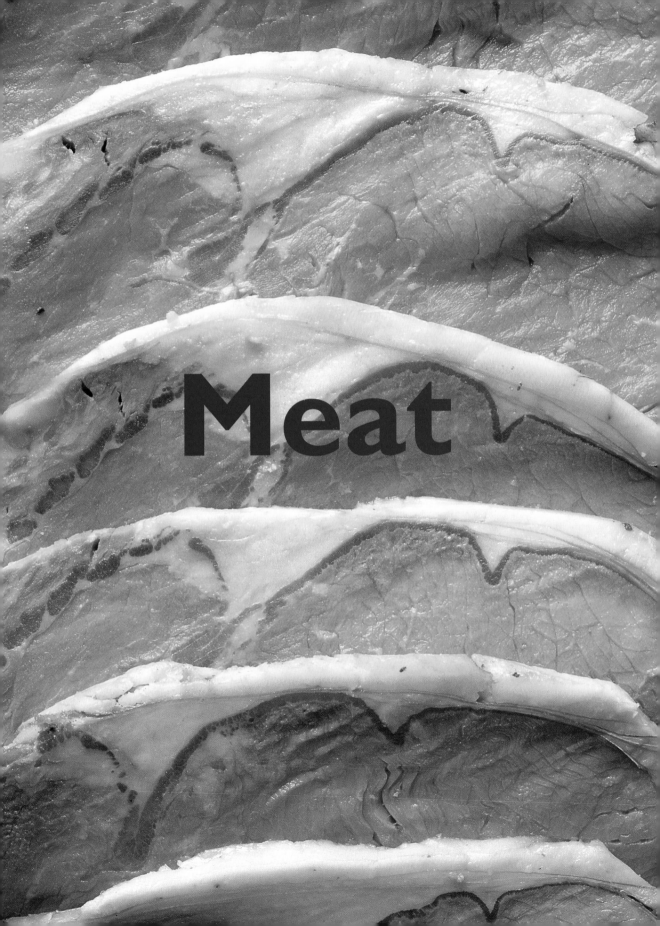

Meat

Grilled Lamb Cutlets with
Buttered Parsley Purée   ‡   serves 4

If I find myself eating in one of those rather old-fashioned hotel restaurants of, say, the 1950s, and am finding it difficult to choose something off the menu that will not spoil my lunch, I will invariably plump for a trio of small grilled lamb cutlets. Béarnaise or freshly made mint sauce are suitable saucings, accompanied by either fried potatoes or *pommes Lyonnaise*. However, this delicious parsley purée lifts the cutlets onto another level of sophistication altogether, yet it is the simplest thing to make.

1 really large bunch of flat-leaf parsley,
   stalks removed, leaves only
100g butter
2 small cloves garlic, peeled and finely
   chopped
grated rind of ½ a lemon
fresh nutmeg

4 tbsp double cream
Maldon sea salt and freshly ground
   black pepper
12 lamb cutlets, trimmed neatly
a little olive oil
watercress to garnish

In a large pan of boiling water, blanch the parsley leaves for 20 seconds. Tip into a sieve and refresh under very cold running water. In a non-reactive (stainless-steel or enamelled) pan, melt the butter, and add the garlic and lemon rind and the blanched parsley leaves. Gently stew for 2 or 3 minutes, grate in the nutmeg (8 rasps) and spoon in the cream. Season. Turn up the heat for a few seconds, boil briefly, then tip into a food processor. Whiz for a minute or so until smooth and unctuous. Tip into a bowl, cover, and keep warm over hot water.

Heat a ribbed cast-iron frying pan until very hot, or use one of those rectangular ribbed stove-top grills, specifically for grilling. A radiant overhead grill will *not* do. This is used for glazing food; in fact, it should be called a glaze, not a grill. Lightly brush the chops with the olive oil, season with pepper and lay on the ribbed surface of the metal. After about 1 minute, turn through 90°, and repeat the process, so as to effect a criss-cross pattern on the surface of the cutlet. Now turn the cutlets onto their fatty edges, for a second or two, to crisp up that fat (slobbery lamb fat is fat from hell). Then turn over onto their other sides and repeat the first step. Sprinkle with a little salt and brush with a little more olive oil. Allow to rest in a *very* low oven for about 5 minutes, to give you fairly rare cutlets; they should be of a uniform thickness – a good 3 cm is about right. This is the correct way to grill meat properly. Do it in batches, and don't overcrowd the pan or grill-top: however hot the receptacle, it will always lose heat when used.

Serve up the cutlets on a hot platter, garnish with some traditional sprigs of watercress and hand the parsley purée separately in a hot bowl.

Lamb Shrewsbury ‡ serves 4

This recipe (after much searching) comes from a 1971 edition of *The Good Food Guide*. It was in those wonderful heady days that small and intimate restaurants were owned and run by extremely gifted amateurs. One such place was Le Carrosse, in Elystan Street, Chelsea. The proprietor was one Geoffrey Sharp, who then went on to open the Grange in Covent Garden. And it was here, in about 1979, that I last remember eating Lamb Shrewsbury.

In these more aggressive days of restauration, when bigger is thought to (sometimes) be better and design more of an allure than content, and fashionable food is fraught with superfluous minutiae, it is heartening to remember a simple dish such as this and also the environment in which it could be found.

12 thick lamb cutlets, trimmed of
    excess fat
1 tbsp dripping or oil
4 tbsp redcurrant jelly
2 tbsp Worcestershire sauce
juice of 1 lemon
110g button mushrooms (I think
    perhaps sliced, although the original
    recipe doesn't require this)

1 scant level tbsp plain flour
275 ml (approx.) vegetable water or
    stock
Maldon sea salt and freshly ground
    black pepper
nutmeg

Using a cast-iron lidded casserole, brown the cutlets in the fat until well coloured and any remaining fat has been rendered. Meanwhile, melt the redcurrant jelly, Worcestershire sauce and lemon juice in another pan.

Preheat the oven to 300°F/150°C/gas mark 2.

Lift out the cutlets and put onto a plate. Set on one side. Now tip out any excess fat, leaving about 1 tbsp behind. Add the mushrooms to this, cook until golden and then tip in the flour. Stir around until the flour has coloured slightly, add the melted jelly mixture and then the vegetable water or stock, and continue to stir until a thickish gravy consistency has been reached (as the lamb cooks, it will thin the gravy). If any lumps form, get at them with a whisk. Season with salt and pepper. Return the meat to the pot, bring up to a gentle simmer and grate over the nutmeg. Put on the lid and cook for about 1½ hours. Check from time to time that the dish is not cooking too fast; if so, turn the temperature down a notch. Serve with potatoes sliced up with onions and baked in the oven in a little stock.

Sliced Pink Cold Roast Lamb, Aubergine Salad and Creamed Goat's Cheese

serves 8–10

The salad is loosely based on Imam Bayeldi, a Middle Eastern way with aubergines which caused that mythical old sultan to faint with pleasure – or, perhaps, overeating. Either way, it is the most delicious of preparations for what many people think of as a 'difficult vegetable'.

This is a really special combination of flavours and textures and although I have given directions for cooking the lamb from scratch, it is, naturally, a very good way of using up leftover cold roast lamb.

1 × 2.5 kg leg of lamb, boned, rolled and tied by the butcher for neat and easy slicing once cooked
6 large garlic cloves, peeled and sliced

into three lengthways
2 tbsp olive oil
Maldon sea salt and freshly ground black pepper

For the aubergine salad:

500g aubergine, cut into 2.5 cm
    cubes
2 medium onions, peeled and finely
    chopped
75 ml olive oil
1 level tbsp salt
1 tsp ground cumin
1 tsp ground cinnamon
½ tsp freshly ground black pepper
8 large tomatoes, peeled and chopped
3 cloves garlic, peeled and chopped

1 tbsp currants
2 tbsp chopped flat-leafed
    parsley
watercress

For the creamed goat's cheese:
300g firm goat's cheese
100g cream cheese
100 ml yogurt
a scraping of nutmeg
Maldon sea salt (if necessary) and
    a good shake of Tabasco

Preheat the oven to 425°F/220°C/gas mark 7.

Make small but deep incisions into the lamb and force the garlic into the holes with your little finger. Smear the joint with the olive oil and season liberally. Roast for 20 minutes in the preheated oven and then turn the temperature down to 325°F/160°C/gas mark 3. Cook for a further hour and then turn the oven off. Leave the door ajar and allow the meat to rest here for 20 minutes before removing from the oven. Put onto a serving platter and pour any resultant juices around the meat. Leave to cool completely, at room temperature.

Using your hands, mix the aubergine with salt and leave to soak for 30 minutes. Meanwhile, fry the onions in 2 tbsp of the olive oil until softened and a pale golden colour. Add the salt and spices, and cook for a couple of minutes, before adding the tomatoes. Stew for about 10 minutes over very gentle heat, adding the garlic for the last three minutes. Now stir in the currants. Rinse the aubergine in plenty of water and pat dry thoroughly in a clean teatowel. Heat the remaining olive oil in a non-stick frying pan until very hot and briskly fry the aubergine until lightly browned. Tip into the onion/tomato mulch and carefully stir in, along with the parsley. Check for seasoning. Spoon into a bowl and allow to cool to room temperature.

If you own a *mouli-légumes* – and you should by now – force the goat's cheese through the finest blade (otherwise push it through a sieve) into a bowl. Add the yogurt and soured cream or crème fraiche, salt (if necessary) and Tabasco and beat well together. Pile into a serving dish, cover with clingfilm and put in the fridge to firm up.

To serve, tuck sprightly bunches of watercress around the lamb before sending to table along with the aubergine and creamed goat's cheese. A crisp green salad may also be served, but I don't really think it necessary, especially if the watercress is of the best. By the way, I think the lamb is best sliced thinly here, rather than in great doorsteps.

Spiced Lamb Meatballs with Tomato and Mint, and Cucumber Salad ‡ serves 4

Essentially, this is an Indian kofta curry served with a cool and creamy cucumber salad – or raita. However, it is a deliciously fragrant preparation, mildly spiced and deeply savoury. The perfect TV dinner, really; only a fork is necessary and, perhaps, a cold glass of beer or two.

For the cucumber salad:
½ cucumber, peeled, deseeded and
  coarsely grated
a pinch of ground cumin
150ml plain yogurt
a little Maldon sea salt

For the meatballs:
4 onions, peeled and finely
  chopped
6 cloves garlic, peeled and finely
  chopped
4 tbsp vegetable oil
700g minced lamb
2 tbsp coriander seeds and 1 tbsp
  cumin seeds, dry roasted together in
  a frying pan until fragrant, then

ground in a pestle and mortar or
  coffee grinder
2 tsp ground turmeric
1 tbsp garam masala
½ tsp chilli powder
1 tsp freshly ground black pepper
1 tsp salt
3 tbsp chopped mint
1 small beaten egg
1 tbsp plain flour
50g butter
½ stick cinnamon
4 cloves
4 ripe tomatoes, peeled and
  chopped
juice of 1 lemon or lime
Maldon sea salt

To make the cucumber salad, mix all the ingredients together thoroughly, put into a bowl and chill in the fridge.

To make the meatballs, fry the onions and garlic in the oil until golden brown. Cool on a plate. Mix into the lamb together with the spices, salt, 1 tbsp mint and egg. Form into balls the size of walnuts, roll in the flour, and fry in the butter in a roomy, shallow pan, until golden brown all over. Put in the cinnamon and cloves and fry for a minute or so with the meat. Now tip in the tomatoes and allow to stew with the meatballs for 20 minutes, until softened and pulpy. Add the lemon or lime juice, the remaining mint and a little salt. Serve straight away with some plain boiled rice and the cucumber salad.

Steak au Poivre   ✢   **serves 2**

This is one of the very first dishes I ever learnt to cook, at the Normandie Restaurant just outside Bury in Lancashire. It was here, as a very junior apprentice, that I truly found my vocation – and initially during the school holidays, aged a tender sixteen years.

This benchmark *Steak au Poivre* is a model of its kind: no cream or any of those silly little pink peppercorns, just much butter and cognac.

1 tbsp white peppercorns
1 tbsp black peppercorns
2 × 180g thick rump steaks
a little Maldon sea salt
1 tbsp olive oil

50g butter, plus a little more if
   necessary
2 tbsp cognac
1 tbsp reduced and jellied beef stock
   (optional)

Coarsely crush the peppercorns in a coffee grinder and put in a sieve. Shake out all the excess powder (this is very important as the powder will make the steaks too hot). Press the pepper into both sides of the steaks and push in well with your fingers. Sprinkle on a little salt now; don't do it before the pepper, as the peppercorns have a tendency to fall off.

Heat the oil in a heavy-bottomed frying pan until smoking. Put in

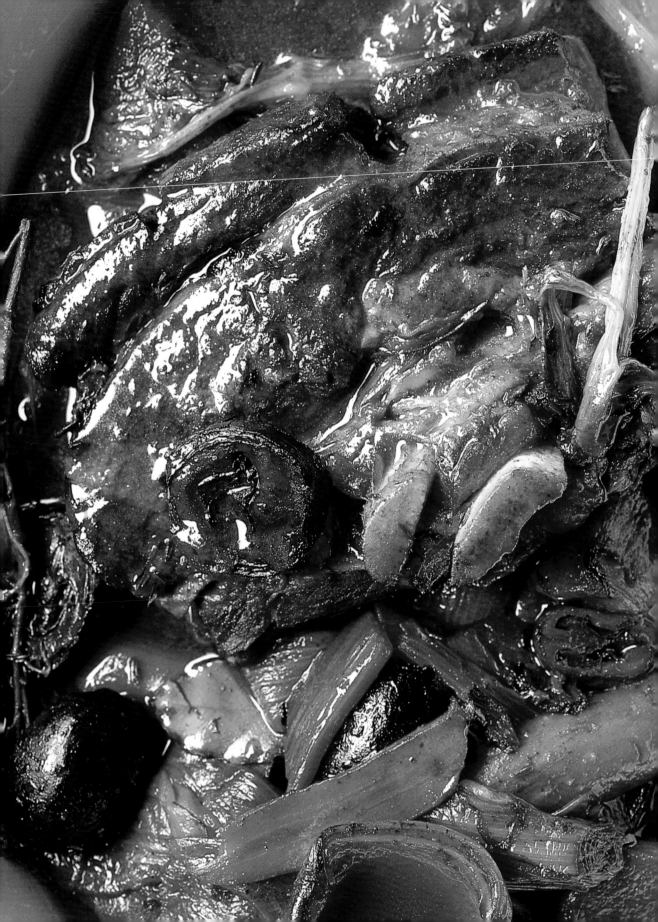

the steaks, leave untouched for a couple of minutes and then turn the heat down a little. Cook for a further 3 minutes or so and then carefully turn over. Turn the heat up again and repeat. Add the butter and allow to foam. Baste with the butter over a gentle heat until it has browned slightly. Remove steaks and keep warm in a low oven with the door ajar. Add the cognac and allow to seethe. What you wish for now is that the cognac and buttery juices will amalgamate to form a sauce. The addition of a little reduced beef stock will help here, or failing that even a splash of water; the idea is to form an emulsion, so a whisk will help. Add more butter too if necessary. Check the sauce for salt and pour over the steaks.

Meat

Braised Beef Brisket with Pickled Walnuts ⁑ serves 4

The resultant meat from this stew emerges melting and very tender. As the meat is better cooked in these two pieces, and on the bone, all that is needed is a spoon to break it up into manageable pieces.

I am very partial indeed to pickled walnuts, and it is a pleasure to be able to include them in this particularly British dish, along with those two other relish ingredients: mushroom ketchup and anchovy essence.

2 x 500g pieces fresh beef brisket
Maldon sea salt and freshly ground
*   black pepper*
3 tbsp plain flour
2 tbsp beef dripping or lard
350g small onions, peeled and
*   quartered*
150g leeks, trimmed, thickly sliced on
*   the diagonal and washed*
150g celery, peeled and thickly sliced

150g small turnips, peeled and
*   quartered*
1 tbsp mushroom ketchup
1 tbsp anchovy essence
6 pickled walnuts, quartered
*   lengthways, and 3 tbsp of their*
*   liquor*
550ml water or stock
2 bay leaves

Left: **Braised Beef Brisket with Pickled Walnuts**

85

Preheat the oven to 275°F/130°C/gas mark 1.

Season the beef all over with salt and pepper then dredge with flour. Melt the dripping or lard in a deep cast-iron lidded casserole dish until very hot. Sear the meat on all surfaces and remove to a plate. Tip off most of the fat and then add the vegetables. Stir around to colour lightly and then add the mushroom ketchup, anchovy essence, pickled walnuts and their liquor and finally the water or stock.

Return the meat to the pot and add the bay leaves. Bring the whole lot up to a gentle simmer, skimming off any froth that generates, and then allow to bubble gently for 10 minutes. Put a lid on and put in the oven. Cook for 1½ to 2 hours, or until completely tender when poked with a skewer. Serve straight from the pot, accompanied by boiled or mashed potatoes, and some extra pickled walnuts as a tracklement.

Onglet Sauté aux Échalotes ⚜ serves 2

Search for a good enterprising local butcher to find the French beef cut *onglet*. It is sometimes referred to here as skirt steak or feather steak. *Bavette* is a good alternative if you have no luck. Otherwise use sirloin. But I still think you should at least ask if the butcher has ever heard of the delicious *onglet*. A word of caution: do try and eat the *onglet* at least pink, but preferably rare, as the meat can toughen considerably when overcooked.

1 tbsp olive oil
freshly ground black pepper
2 x 180g pieces of onglet
40g butter
4 shallots, chopped fairly coarsely

a tiny squeeze of lemon juice
2 tbsp dry white wine
Maldon sea salt or a couple of finely
*   chopped anchovies (optional)*
½ tbsp chopped parsley

Take a heavy-bottomed frying pan and heat the olive oil until smoking. Pepper the *onglet* and quickly fry for about 2 minutes on each side until seared deep brown (for rare). Put onto a plate and keep warm (as for *Steak au Poivre*, page 83). Add the butter to the pan and allow to foam. Throw in the shallots and cook gently until golden brown; this may take up to 5 minutes. Squeeze in the lemon juice and add the white wine. Allow to bubble until syrupy and then season (the anchovies, by the way, are not as odd sounding as you might think; their salty – rather than fishy – flavour has always been well regarded when partnered with meat, particularly lamb). Stir in the parsley and pour over the meat.

Lamb Tjitske ‡ serves 4

One of the more remarkable dishes that I ever had the pleasure of eating (circa 1979), was a trio of spiced and grilled lamb cutlets, cooked by the McCoy brothers at their eponymous restaurant at the Tontine, Staddlebridge, in North Yorkshire. The dish is called Lamb Tjitske, and was described on the wondrously eclectic menu (the McCoys did eclecticism in food long ago, as a matter of choice and understanding, embracing it purely because it excited them) as having 'Javanese overtones'. They also did a chocolate dessert called Choc-o-block Stanley, named after the man who used to deliver their evening paper. On each occasion, he would ask if they were busy; their reply was always, 'Oh, chock-a-block, Stanley! Chock-a-block!' It knocks the romance behind the naming of Peach Melba into a cocked hat, don't you think?

Anyway, here's the recipe for Lamb Tjitske, by courtesy of Tom, Peter and Eugene McCoy. Thanks, lads.

12 plump lamb cutlets, not fatty chops (ask the butcher to cut them from the best end)

For the marinade:
150ml light soy sauce
50ml sesame oil
1 large clove garlic, peeled and crushed
half a small onion, peeled and chopped

50g piece fresh ginger, peeled and sliced
juice of 1 orange
juice of 1 lemon
25g brown sugar
1 tsp ground coriander
1 tsp ground cumin
1 tsp ground turmeric
½ tsp cayenne pepper

Liquidize all the ingredients for the marinade and then pour through a sieve. Lay the cutlets in a suitable dish and pour over the marinade. Move the cutlets around with your hands so that they are evenly coated with the mixture. Cover with clingfilm or foil and put into the fridge for 24 hours. Turn them occasionally.

Heat a stove-top ribbed grill, preferably, or failing that a large heavy-bottomed frying pan (a charcoal fire, however, will give the most perfect and authentic results). Lift out the chops from the marinade and shake off excess liquid. Lay onto a metal tray or plate, ready for cooking. Heat the grill or frying pan till really hot and then dribble over a film of oil (any old oil will do). Allow to smoke and then grill the chops. Keep at a high heat throughout the cooking process, which should not be more than about 3–4 minutes on each side. It is intentional that they will become slightly blackened, but the resultant pink inside contrasts winningly with the carbonized exterior. Serve with an interesting salad. The brothers McCoy used to do something called Salad Incredible. The name now sounds a bit naff, but it really did have an incredible taste. And d'you know, I don't think there was a rocket leaf in sight.

Hash ⁜ serves 4

A hash is the perfect brunch dish and seen all over America in the home, coffee shops, delis and diners. I cannot think of anything nicer for New Year's Day or a Saturday late lunch, for example, and would go even further to suggest it as a weekend breakfast dish. Serve a jug of spicy Bloody Marys or a tray of Bullshots alongside as the ideal accompaniments.

25g butter
a little freshly grated nutmeg
100g diced bacon
225g onions, peeled and chopped
500g cooked meat (beef, lamb, pork or
*   turkey, for example)*

400g potatoes, peeled, cut into cubes
*   and simmered until tender*
2 tbsp chopped parsley (mint is a good
*   addition if you are using lamb;*
*   sage if it is pork)*
Maldon sea salt

a few good shakes of Tabasco and   *4 eggs*
   Worcester sauce

Melt the butter in a large, preferably non-stick frying pan. Fry the bacon until crisp and then add the onions. Cook for a few minutes until soft. Now tip in the meat and potatoes. Turn the heat down a little and further cook for around 20 minutes. The idea is for the whole mass to develop a crust, which is then turned back into itself so that the new surfaces form a new crust, and so on. A wooden spatula is ideal here, so that you can lift up and turn the hash on a fairly constant basis. But you must allow that crust to develop before turning; too much movement will result in a dull and soggy mess.

Add the nutmeg, parsley and other chosen herbs halfway through the cooking and then shake in the Tabasco and Worcester sauces towards the end, together with some salt. Divide into four portions and put onto hot plates. Top each serving with either a fried or a poached egg. Serve straight away.

Polpettine   serves 4

Polpettine are the Italian meatball. But they are not just any old lump of minced meat in sauce. The flavourings that I like to use, and add to the minced meat, are suitably savoury too, using chopped anchovy, lemon rind, Parmesan and fresh herbs. Serve up with generous amounts of buttery mashed potato here, or soft and equally lubricated polenta (nice in the left to set, cut and grilled form), to achieve the most pleasing result.

75g fresh white breadcrumbs
5 tbsp milk
500g minced veal
200g piece belly pork, minced, rind
   discarded
1 large egg, beaten

grated rind of 1 lemon
2 tbsp chopped flat-leaf parsley
1 tbsp chopped oregano or marjoram
50g freshly grated Parmesan
10–12 anchovy fillets, cut into pieces
a little plain flour

3–4 tbsp pure olive oil
50g butter
275ml dry white wine

6 tbsp passata (fresh pure pasteurized tomato pulp, sieved, sold in cartons)
1 clove garlic, peeled and chopped

In a large bowl mix the first nine ingredients together well. Form into small balls about 4cm in diameter. Then, with your finger, push a small piece of anchovy into the centre and then re-form, pressing lightly between your fingers to flatten slightly (depending upon your love of anchovies, up to half a fillet may be inserted). You should end up with about 5–6 meatballs per serving. Roll in the flour and set aside on a tray.

Take a large, deep-sided frying pan and in it melt the oil and butter. Heat until foaming and then carefully add the meatballs in one layer. Turn the heat down and gently fry until nicely coloured on one side. Turn over and continue frying. Once the other sides are coloured too, tip the pan slightly and remove most of the fat with a large spoon. Pour in about a third of the wine and allow to bubble. Shake the pan occasionally and allow the wine to reduce to almost nothing. Pour in more of the wine and turn the meatballs over again. Cover and simmer for 20 minutes on a very low heat.

Remove the lid and take the meatballs from the pan with a slotted spoon. Put onto a serving dish and place in a warmed oven. Turn the heat up to high and add the rest of the wine, the passata and the garlic. Reduce until saucy and sort of syrupy. Spoon over the *polpettine*, strew with a little more chopped parsley and serve. A little squeeze of lemon juice over the meat adds zing.

Vitello Tonnato ‡ serves 10–12

There have been so many recipes published for this cold Italian favourite that I almost feel guilty about giving the recipe once more. However, it can often be slapdash in the making and some methods that I have read are a bit rum, to say the least. Carefully made, purely for the purpose (not leftovers), *Vitello Tonnato* is, quite simply, one of the very best cold meat dishes it is possible to eat.

Left: Polpettine

Try to find a selective butcher who will purchase good veal in the first place. I have found that a small rump of veal, boned, rolled and tied up is the best cut for this dish. It will cost one dearly, but at the same time will feed about 10–12 people. So why not do it for a large weekend lunch, out of doors, and eat it with a Pea and Rice Salad (page 149)?

4–5 tbsp olive oil	For the sauce:
Maldon sea salt and freshly ground	1 x 200g can olive-oil-packed tuna
black pepper	2 x 50g tins anchovies
2–2.5 kg boned, rolled and tied rump	juice of 1 large lemon
of veal	a few squirts of Tabasco
1 glass white wine	275 ml light, pure olive oil
1 glass water	(not extra-virgin)
2 sprigs rosemary	a little Maldon sea salt (if needed)
2 cloves garlic, peeled and lightly	2 tbsp capers, drained and squeezed dry
crushed	2 tbsp extra-virgin olive oil
	watercress

Preheat the oven to 300°F/150°C/gas mark 2.

Using a heavy-bottomed, cast-iron casserole dish with a lid (Le Creuset is best), heat the olive oil until lightly smoking. Season the meat (lightly with the salt) and brown it on all sides in the oil. Carefully tip out any excess fat and pour in the wine and water. Bring up to a simmer and pop in the rosemary and garlic. Put on the lid and place in the oven for 20 minutes. Remove and turn the veal over. Cook for a further 20 minutes. Take out of the oven and tweak with your fingers. It should feel tight and bouncy. However, if the meat still has a slackness about it, put it back for another 10 minutes or so. Once removed from the oven, leave the lid on and put in a cool place for a further 20 minutes. Lift out the piece of meat, put on a large plate, allow to rest and cool completely. Then put in the fridge. Meanwhile, strain the resultant juices through a fine sieve into a clean pan and lift off any surface fat with kitchen paper. Reduce by half, but keep tasting as you go for excessive saltiness. Pour into a bowl and cool, then put in the fridge.

To make the sauce, tip the tuna and anchovies into a liquidizer. Blend until very smooth with the lemon juice and Tabasco. Start to add the olive oil in a thin stream as if you are making mayonnaise. When the mixture starts to become thick, add – a little at a time – some of the meat juices so as to loosen the mixture. Play around a bit here: oil, meat juices, perhaps a little water, oil, meat juices, etc., etc. The final consistency should be one of thickish salad cream; just pourable.

Remove the string from the veal when cold, and slice thinly (it should be pink). Take a large, preferably white, oval dish or plate. Lay the slices in an overlapping arrangement and carefully spoon over the sauce. Sprinkle over the capers evenly and, in a willy-nilly way, finally drizzle over the extra-virgin olive oil. Decorate with some cool and sprightly watercress.

Sliced Crisp Belly Pork with Greens ‡

serves 6

Ask the butcher to finely score the skin of the pork and to remove the bones, which should be chopped up into smaller pieces and taken home with you. The greens to use are a matter for you. If you wish to be authentic, use Chinese *bok choy* or mustard greens. Otherwise, choose young spinach leaves or Swiss chard. Start the recipe the day before you want to eat it.

*700g fatty belly pork, scored and
    boned
1 tbsp Chinese five-spice mixture
2 tsp freshly ground white
    pepper
1 level tbsp Maldon sea salt*

For the stock:
*1 litre water
100ml soy sauce (Kikomann is
    a good brand)*

*100ml dry sherry
1 tbsp honey
5–6 slices fresh ginger
1 small bunch spring onions,
    chopped
3 cloves garlic, bashed
1 tsp dried chilli flakes
4 strips orange rind
bones from the pork*

To finish:

6 *heads* bok choy, *or 12 leaves (including stalks) of Swiss chard, or 1.5 kg spinach*

a few slices of green and red chilli sprigs coriander

Set a large pot of water to boil (about 5 litres). Lay the belly pork on a cooling rack over a deep tray, skin side uppermost. With a ladle, pour the boiling water over the skin until it is all used up. Discard the used water. Turn the belly pork over onto a large tray and rub the meat with the five-spice mixture and pepper, working them in well with the tips of your fingers. Now turn over once more and rub the salt into the skin. Hang the meat up to dry in a cool and draughty place overnight.

Preheat the oven to 475°F/250°C/gas mark 9.

Mix all the stock ingredients in a bowl and pour into a deep roasting tin. Over this, suspend the cooling rack you used before and place the pork upon it, skin side up. Place at the top of the oven and roast for 10 minutes. Turn the temperature down to 350°F/180°C/gas mark 4 and cook for a further 45 minutes. Now take the pork out, top up the liquid with water if it has reduced too much, and turn the oven to full temperature once more. Once back up to temperature, return the pork to the oven and roast for a final 10 minutes or so. This strange method does seem to have a magical effect of producing a fabulously crisp skin (I first read about this method in one of Ken Hom's highly educational Chinese cookery books).

Allow the pork to cool on the rack, set over another tin and strain the liquid from the roasting tin into a small pan. Keep warm.

Steam (or briefly boil) the *bok choy*, Swiss chard or spinach until tender and keep warm. Slice the *bok choy* or Swiss chard into manageable pieces, but if you are using spinach, leave as it is. Place on a serving dish. Using a sharp serrated knife, cut the pork as thinly as you can. Lay over the chosen greens in overlapping slices and spoon over some of the roasting juices (any left over can be used again; keep in the freezer until the next time). Sprinkle over the chilli and decorate with sprigs of coriander.

Note: The dish is often best served at room temperature.

Grilled Pork Chop with Kidney and Bacon, and Garlic Butter ‡ serves 4

Savoury butters are one of the nicest ways to lubricate and embellish grilled meats and fish. This pork chop, with its bacon-wrapped kidney, is transformed by a little fat disc of garlic butter, together with a goodly smear of the same secreted between the roasted bacon and kidney. This will provide a further emollient to an invariably dry piece of rarely cooked offal.

Another suitable compound butter here is an amalgam of sage and onion, or perhaps paprika and dill mixed with a further addition of sour cream to both lighten it and introduce a faintly Hungarian note when served with a piece of pork.

Note: It is not practical to make small quantities of a savoury butter. Freeze that which you do not use.

For the garlic butter:
250g unsalted butter, softened to room temperature
25g peeled garlic, as fresh as possible (the new season's stuff is particularly good here), very finely chopped
40g flat parsley leaves, very finely chopped
25ml Pernod or Ricard
1 level tsp salt
¼ tsp freshly ground black pepper
a generous pinch of cayenne
6 drops Tabasco

To finish:
2 pig's kidneys, skin and core removed
freshly ground black pepper
8 thin slices flat pancetta
4 plump free-range pork chops, rind removed
Maldon sea salt
a little olive oil
watercress

First make the garlic butter. Put all the ingredients into the bowl of an electric mixer (or in a roomy bowl and use an electric hand whisk or spatula) and beat together until smooth. Dampen a sheet of greaseproof paper and spoon the butter onto it in a rough log shape. Roll up into a tighter log, twisting the ends to form a sort of Christmas cracker. Then

roll this up even tighter, using a sheet of strong kitchen foil, once again twisting the ends. Put to chill in the fridge.

Preheat the oven to 375°F/190°C/gas mark 5. Also heat a ribbed, stove-top grill pan until it is very hot indeed.

Season the kidneys with pepper. Lay out the *pancetta* on a chopping board in two sets of four, slightly overlapping. Spread each quartet with a thin layer of garlic butter and then lay a kidney at one end. Roll up the bacon around the kidney, making sure that the join is underneath. Carefully place into a largish roasting tin (the chops are going to end up in here for a few minutes too) and put in the oven. Roast until the bacon has become crisp and good-looking – about 15 minutes.

As soon as the kidney has gone into the oven, season and lightly oil the chops. Slap onto the grill and burnish well on both sides – about 5 minutes. Do not cook through, however, as they are now going to sit alongside the kidneys in the oven, to finish cooking there. Remove the kidneys when they feel bouncy to the touch, put onto a warm plate and cover. Leave to relax for 5 minutes or so.

Once the chops are done, remove also and put onto 4 hot plates. Slice the kidneys into six, across their length, and garnish each chop with 3 slices. Spoon over any juices that have collected in the roasting tin and pop a slice of garlic butter onto each chop. Decorate with watercress.

Grilled Sausages and Mashed Potatoes, with Onion and Apple Sauces ‡

serves 4

This was one of those favourite family lunches that we invariably had on a Saturday at home, sitting around the kitchen table. And if my memory serves me well, it was also usually after the folks had been in the pub, having left my brother and me in the car with a packet of crisps and a tomato juice.

As perfect a meal as any I can recall: grilled pork sausages, mashed potato, apple sauce and a creamy onion sauce. Initially, one might think it

Left: **Grilled Pork Chop with Kidney and Bacon, and Garlic Butter**

curious that such a simple conglomeration could be so 'gastronomic' – for want of a better description. But really, it is all to do with knowing what tastes good with what.

For the apple sauce:
2 large Bramley apples, peeled and
  sliced
3 tbsp water
2 cloves
2 tbsp caster sugar
scant juice of ½ a small lemon

For the mashed potatoes:
1 kg floury potatoes, peeled and cut
  into chunks
Maldon sea salt
75 ml creamy milk
75 g butter
freshly ground white pepper
nutmeg

For the onion sauce:
200 ml milk
1 bay leaf
2 sprigs thyme
Maldon sea salt
25 g butter
2 medium onions, peeled and very
  finely sliced
1 level tbsp plain flour
75 ml single cream
freshly grated nutmeg
freshly ground black pepper

To finish:
12 sausages, the best ones you know,
  obviously, but of the commercially
  produced brands, I like Porkinson's
  the best

To make the apple sauce, put everything into a small pan and cook gently for about 20–25 minutes until the apples have collapsed and the mixture has become a chunky purée; I personally don't like it too smooth. Pour into a bowl to cool to room temperature.

To make the mashed potatoes, boil the potatoes in salted water until cooked. Meanwhile, warm together the milk and butter in a small pan. Drain the potatoes well (dry out in the oven if they seem excessively wet). Pass the potatoes through a *mouli-légumes* or potato ricer. Beat the potato with a manual or electric hand whisk, adding the milk and butter mixture in a thin stream. Season with pepper and nutmeg and check for salt. When all has been added, give the mash a final energetic beating to lighten it.

To make the onion sauce, heat together the milk, bay leaf, thyme and a little salt. Simmer for a few minutes, remove from the heat, cover and allow the flavours to mingle for 10 minutes. In another pan, melt the butter and add the onions. Cook very gently until completely soft but uncoloured. Stir in the flour and gently cook together for a minute or two. Strain the milk into the onions, stirring continuously until thickened. On the lowest possible heat, preferably with a heat-diffuser pad, set the sauce to cook. Stir, from time to time, with a wooden spoon and then add the cream, nutmeg, and pepper, mix in thoroughly, check for salt and cook for a further 2 minutes.

Fry the sausages in the usual way, until well crusted and brown, and serve with the mash and sauces.

Poultry *and* Game

Roast Goose Stuffed with Mashed Potato ‡ serves 6

Of all the recipes over the last four years, this one has been the most sought after. Last Christmas a keen cook I know telephoned in a flat spin from her house in the Dordogne. She had lost the recipe and, having had much success with it the year before, was desperate to repeat it. A fax was dispatched and reached the depths of the Dordogne, happily just in the nick of time. It is a great pleasure to know that recipes have become part of someone's annual repertoire – and particularly pleasing, considering that the goose recipe was the very first piece of copy I was asked to file for the *Independent*, by Emily Green. So here it is once more.

I have to admit that the idea is not original. The late Peter Langan introduced this way of cooking his goose to the menu at Langan's Brasserie, where it makes regular appearances around Christmas time. Incidentally, I would also like to say here that Langan's remains one of the most wonderful restaurants in the world: always full, always buzzy, genial service from real waiters and one of the most agreeable dining rooms anywhere. And the food is spot on, fitting and unsullied by fad or fashion. Long may it please and prosper.

I think that the Chinese method of pouring boiling water over the surface of a duck or goose is the best way to achieve a crisp skin. The skin of the bird must first be punctured many times with the point of a thin skewer or sharp knife. These little holes then open up on contact with the boiling water and allow the subcutaneous layer of fat to flow out. The bird should then be allowed to dry.

If you have an electric fan, hang up the bird, directing the flow of air directly onto it. Do this by an open window and leave for a few hours, or preferably overnight. The original instruction two years ago was the simpler method of just putting it on a wire rack by the same open window, turning over from time to time. The fan method, however, works even better, so if you have one use it. The end result of all this palaver should be moist flesh and parchmentlike skin without the usual goo. Believe me, it *is* worth doing.

Before giving the goose this treatment remove the great gobbets of fat that lie just inside the cavity, attached to the skin. Put them in a pot with 2 tbsp oil and place on a very low light. Allow to melt. Goose fat is precious and keeps for ages in the fridge. As the goose is roasting, tip off the fat that constantly drips into this pot. You will be amazed at the amount collected. Use it regularly – to fry potatoes in with garlic and parsley, for instance.

Maldon sea salt and plenty of freshly ground black pepper
1 goose, dressed weight about 5kg or so, with giblets
1.5 kg potatoes, peeled, chopped into large chunks and rinsed thoroughly
4 onions, peeled and coarsely chopped
50g goose or duck fat
2 cloves garlic, peeled and finely chopped
1 tbsp chopped sage leaves
grated rind of 2 lemons

For the gravy:
4 rashers of streaky bacon, chopped
25g goose or duck fat
1 goose neck bone, coarsely chopped
1 goose gizzard, cleaned (ask your butcher) and coarsely chopped
1 onion, peeled and chopped
1 carrot, peeled and chopped
2 sticks of celery, chopped
2 tbsp calvados
150ml Madeira
300ml strong chicken stock
1 dsp redcurrant jelly
1 tsp arrowroot, slaked with a little water

Preheat the oven to 425°F/220°C/gas mark 7.

Rub salt all over the goose and sprinkle some inside the cavity as well, with some pepper. Boil the potatoes in salted water until tender, drain well and coarsely mash them. Fry the onions in the goose or duck fat until golden brown. Add the garlic and stir into the mashed potato along with the sage, lemon rind and pepper. Pack this mixture into the cavity of the goose.

Now put the goose in a roomy roasting tin, still on its wire rack, and place in the oven. Roast for 30 minutes and then turn the temperature down to 350°F/180°C/gas mark 4. Cook the goose for a further 2½ hours or so. This is one of those rare instances when basting is not required, as the more the fat runs off the goose, the better. (Remember to keep pouring it off from the tray during cooking.)

Whilst the goose is cooking, make the gravy. Fry the bacon in the goose or duck fat in a heavy-bottomed saucepan until crisp and brown. Add the goose neck bone and gizzard and cook until well coloured; ditto the vegetables. Pour off any excess fat and add the calvados and Madeira. Bring to the boil and reduce until syrupy. Pour in the chicken stock and redcurrant jelly and simmer for 30 minutes. Strain through a fine sieve into a clean pan. Allow to settle and lift off any fat that is float-ing on the surface with some kitchen paper. Whisk in the arrowroot and bring the gravy back to a simmer until clear and slightly thickened. Keep warm. Note: Do not boil, or the arrowroot can break down and thin the gravy.

When the goose is cooked, remove from the oven and allow to rest for 15 minutes or so before carving. And why not serve some of those fried potatoes cooked in goose fat that I mentioned earlier, as well as the potato stuffing? The contrast is really good. Any other green vegetable is a matter for you, but an accompaniment of big bunches of watercress is jolly nice.

Stuffed Goose's Neck ⁺

serves 3–4 as a first course, or 6 as a hot accompaniment to Roast Goose Stuffed with Mashed Potato

You might be interested to know that I threw this together in a matter of minutes. This is not a brag, a crow or in the style of a Martha 'I know this sounds a touch tricky and I can do it much better than you anyway but you must *try*' Stewart recipe, it is just that it really was so easy to do.

Life is certainly not too short to stuff a goose's neck. Apart from any-thing, you already have some of the ingredients: heart and liver (or at least you should have), and the goose neck skin. Make sure you request of the butcher or game dealer that he cuts the neck as close to the goose's head as possible.

the goose liver plus enough duck or
*   chicken liver (or indeed raw foie*
*   gras if you can find some) to*
*   measure up to 200g*
the goose heart
200g rindless belly pork
50g streaky bacon or pancetta
200g duck breast (available very easily
*   in supermarkets now), skin*
*   removed*

1 small clove peeled garlic
1 tsp thyme leaves
1 tbsp chopped parsley
¼ tsp salt and plenty of freshly ground
*   black pepper*
¼ tsp ground allspice
1 small egg, beaten
40g fresh breadcrumbs
2 tbsp armagnac

Cut the neck skin away from the goose as close as you dare to the bird itself (it will look like a huge flap after the goose has been dressed, which you would normally fold under it before roasting). Lay this flap out flat on a chopping board and slice off any very thick lumps of fat (put these in a pan with other lumps of melting fat that have been removed from just inside the goose's bottom – see the previous recipe. Place between two sheets of greaseproof paper and carefully beat flat with a rolling pin or meat bat. Place in the fridge to firm up, still between the paper.

Mince together the livers (and foie gras if using), heart, pork, bacon or *pancetta*, duck breast and garlic, once, through the large-hole blade of a mincer, and stir in the remaining ingredients.

Remove the goose skin from the fridge and peel off the paper. Lay out with the inside of the skin uppermost. Spoon the minced mixture onto the skin and roll up loosely. Stitch the skin together along the join with needle and a double thickness of black thread (easier to see). Do not make the package too tight as the skin will shrink as it cooks. Place in a deep pan that will hold it neatly and strain over some of the goose fat until the 'sausage' is well covered. Poach very, very gently – just a few bubbles – for 1 hour.

If serving hot, leave in the fat for 10 minutes before carving into thick slices, remembering to remove the thread before doing so. If serving cold, leave to cool in the fat and then place the whole thing in the fridge for anything up to 2–3 weeks. Remove from the fat, scrape off any excess and slice thinly like a pâté and serve with Cumberland sauce or a fruity chutney.

Braised Chicken Thighs with Endives and Bacon ‡ serves 4

This is deeply savoury and produces a lovely amalgam of flavours. It is almost complete in itself, but a spoonful or two of smooth mashed potato on the plate might be just perfect for a sloppy finish. Endives are a really good idea when cooked with braised poultry or feathered game; pheasant is particularly suitable here.

2 tbsp olive oil
50g butter
Maldon sea salt and freshly ground
    black pepper
8 chicken thighs
175g smoked bacon, in the piece, rind
    removed and diced into 1cm chunks

8 small endives, trimmed, and with the
    solid base of each neatly cut out
juice of 2 lemons
4 tbsp good jellied chicken stock
    (see Chicken Broth, page 2)
1 small glass dry white wine
2 tbsp coarsely chopped flat-leaf parsley

Preheat the oven to 350°F/180°C/gas mark 4.

Heat the olive oil and butter in a roomy frying pan until foaming. Season the thighs and gently cook on both sides until a rich golden colour. Transfer to a shallow, heavy-duty casserole dish (such as Le Creuset). Add the bacon to the frying pan and cook in the chicken fat until browned. Remove and put with the chicken. Now introduce the endives into the fat and cook gently all over until evenly browned. Tip out all but 1 tbsp of fat, pour in the lemon juice and allow to amalgamate and cook very gently for 5 minutes. Put together with the chicken, the endive juices and all. Pour the chicken stock and wine into the frying pan and boil until reduced by half. Stir in the parsley. Pour over the chicken and endive and place in the oven. Cook, covered, for about 40 minutes, until tender, moist, and smelling wonderful.

Pheasant Stewed with Cider and Calvados ‡ serves 4

Sometimes called *Faisan à la Vallée d'Auge*, after a particular region of Normandy famed for its calvados and, therefore, apples. Much cream is also readily available in this region too, as you might well know. The combination is a rich one, and all the better for that, in these overly health-conscious times. Choose hen birds, as they are more tender than big cocks.

50g butter
Maldon sea salt and freshly ground
    black pepper
2 small hen pheasants, jointed into
    4 breasts and 4 legs
75g smoked bacon, diced
4 large shallots, peeled and coarsely
    chopped

100g white button mushrooms,
    thickly sliced
50ml calvados
300ml dry cider
1 sprig rosemary
juice of ½ a lemon
300ml whipping cream

Melt the butter in a large, preferably cast-iron, casserole pot. Season the pheasant pieces, and when the butter is foaming and just about to colour put them in and gently fry on both sides until pale golden. Remove and put on a plate. Add the bacon, shallots and mushrooms and cook until lightly coloured – about 5–10 minutes. Tip the pot and remove as much fat as you can. Put back the pheasant pieces, turn the heat up a little and pour in the calvados. Allow it to bubble, light with a match and stand clear. Once the flames have subsided, pour in the cider and bring up to a gentle simmer. Tuck in the rosemary sprig, put on the lid, slightly ajar, and simmer very gently for 30 minutes – if you have one of those heat-diffuser pads, use it, or you may wish to cook the pheasant in a low oven (300°F/150°C/gas mark 2). Turn the pieces from time to time.

Lift out the pheasant, shake off any bits of vegetable and put them back onto a plate for a moment. Strain the cooking liquor into a bowl through a sieve, pressing hard on the vegetable matter, and then return the resultant juice to the casserole pot. Add the lemon juice. Bring to the boil, then simmer until reduced by about three-quarters and the consistency has become syrupy. Add the cream and whisk together. Cook for about 5 minutes until creamy and slightly thickened. Now return the pheasant to the pot and further simmer, very gently, until the sauce is unctuous and generously coats the pheasant pieces.

Serve with some chunks of apple (Cox's, perhaps) cooked until soft in a little butter, sugar, a squeeze of lemon and a little more of that calvados.

Crisp Fried Chicken with Chillies and Garlic ‡ serves 4

This perky little number owes its provenance to a tiny little Malaysian restaurant called Melati, just off Piccadilly Circus, in London's celebrated West End. I first ate it here with Ian Bates and Jeremy Lee, two of my very favourite chefs who used to work for me in the kitchens at Bibendum. 'You have just got to have this,' urged Ian. 'Yes, it's just fab, darling,' screeched Jerry. It was refreshing to hear them order me around for a change. The version that follows is my interpretation.

4 large chicken legs (thigh and drumstick together), or 8 thighs
6 tbsp soy sauce
3 tbsp dry sherry
2 tbsp ginger syrup from a jar of stem ginger
oil for frying

2 tbsp cornflour
8 cloves garlic, peeled and sliced
5 large red chillies, deseeded and sliced
Maldon sea salt
lime or lemon wedges
chopped coriander

Cut the chicken legs in two at the joint. Chop each thigh into 3 pieces and each drumstick in 2. Do not skin the meat. Put in a shallow dish. Mix together the soy sauce, sherry and ginger syrup and pour over the chicken. Leave to marinate for at least 2 hours, turning the pieces occasionally.

Pour enough oil in a wok or deep (preferably non-stick) frying pan, to come to a depth of about 0.5cm. Put onto a moderate flame and heat up. Lift out the chicken pieces from the marinade and pat dry. Dip

in the cornflour, coating the pieces well, and place on a plate. Heat until almost smoking and add the chicken pieces, but don't overcrowd; fry in two batches if necessary. Keeping the heat up, turn the chicken when it has become crusted in places and keep frying until all surfaces are a deep golden brown. Put the chicken pieces on a plate and then add the garlic and chillies to the hot oil. Fry until crisp and slightly browned. Return the chicken to the pan, and give a final toss together with the garlic, chillies and a little salt, so that all is well mixed together. Turn into a colander to drain off any excess oil. Tip onto a heated serving platter, garnish with the lime or lemon wedges and the coriander. Eat with a watercress and beansprout salad, dressed with a little sesame oil and rice vinegar.

Guinea Fowl with Mushrooms, Celery and Tarragon   ‡   serves 4

Fresh wild mushrooms are becoming more and more widely available in good greengrocers and the better supermarkets. If you manage to find some good specimens, then feel free to use them in this recipe – the little orange *girolles* would be particularly fitting. However, cultivated mushrooms will be absolutely fine, but go for the slightly open-cupped variety that have a sort of browny-pink look about them. Don't be tempted by those horrid shiitake fungi, though; personally, I think the flavour very odd and not worth the expense.

1 guinea fowl
25 g butter
1 tbsp olive oil
Maldon sea salt and freshly ground
  black pepper
2 tbsp Pernod
about 10 medium sized mushrooms,
  thickly sliced

5 small and tender celery stalks,
  peeled
1 large glass white wine
1 tbsp chopped tarragon
a squeeze of lemon juice
150 ml whipping cream
a few extra tarragon leaves

Left: Crisp Fried Chicken with Chillies and Garlic

Remove the legs (drumstick and thigh in one piece) and then the breasts from the guinea fowl (make a good stock with the carcass). Separate the drumstick from the thigh with a sharp knife and cut each breast into two roughly equal-sized pieces. You will now have 8 parts. Melt the butter and olive oil in a shallow solid-bottomed stew pan (preferably one with a lid), season the guinea fowl and gently fry until golden. Tip off most of the fat and pour over the Pernod. Light with a match and allow the flames to die down. Remove the guinea fowl to a plate. Add the mushrooms and celery to the pan juices and stew gently for about 10 minutes until lightly coloured. Put back the guinea fowl, pour over the wine and stir in the tarragon. Put onto a very low light, cover, and allow to stew for about 30 minutes.

Now lift out the meat, place in a deep serving dish and keep warm in a low oven, covered with foil. Turn the heat up to full and reduce the winey juices and vegetables until the surrounding liquid has become syrupy. Add the squeeze of lemon and stir in the cream. Bring up to a simmer and cook until unctuous and of a coating consistency. Spoon over the guinea fowl and generously sprinkle with tarragon leaves. Serve with plainly boiled potatoes.

Jugged Hare and Forcemeat Balls ‡

serves 3–4

My first memories of hare are so powerfully vivid and off-putting that I am eternally surprised I ever took to the beast. However, I suppose it takes a great deal more than a rank smell and blood in one's face to push a dedicated cook and naturally inquisitive eater out of the running, especially when the culinary learning curve is only just beginning its upward arc.

The smell, to a small boy, of a jugged hare cooking, thrust upon a relatively uninitiated nasal passage, is one of such putrefaction that it beggars belief. What *can* Mother be cooking now? The stench emanating from the bottom oven of the Aga was of such strength that it was impossible not to imagine that she might have finally found a way of cooking what

Bodger went in the garden to do. *Phwoor!* was the immediate exclamation from my childish vocabulary; as pertinent a clamour to this simmering dish as to the 'silent but deadlies' in the class room, after having recently eaten mince in the school canteen.

The following recipe for 'stewed hare' comes from *The Best of Eliza Acton* (Penguin Books, 1974), but seems to be the nearest sounding dish to the one my mother used to make. If you are lucky enough to get a quantity of blood when you collect your hare, stir it into the hot stew five minutes before you dish it up. Also make sure you have all bits of the hare's offal intact. Words within brackets that occasionally occur throughout the recipe are my more modern instructions or explanations to the original text.

1 hare, skinned
2–3 tbsp flour
50g butter
150g streaky bacon or pancetta, *chopped*
1 litre gravy (see recipe method)

pithless rind from half a large lemon
1 dsp rice flour
2 tbsp mushroom ketchup
½ tsp ground mace
cayenne
salt

'Cut the hare down into joints (legs are removed through a ball and socket joint, shoulders directly through a thin membrane and the saddle needs to be hewn from the ribcage with a heavy knife; similarly, the bony part near the tail also should be removed with a swift chop) dividing the largest, flour (dredged in) and brown it slightly in butter with some bits of lean ham (streaky bacon or *pancetta* would be fine), pour to them by degrees a pint and a half of gravy (rich chicken stock simmered with the ribcage, tail piece, livers, hearts and lungs of the hare, all chopped up, for about 1 hour and strained), and stew the hare very gently for an hour and a half to two hours: when it is about one third done add the very thin rind of half a large lemon, and ten minutes before it is served stir to it a large dessertspoonful (rounded dessertspoonful) of rice flour (arrowroot, cornflour or potato flour – *fécule*), smoothly mixed with two tablespoonsful of good mushroom catsup (mushroom ketchup), a quarter of a teaspoonful or more of mace, and something less of cayenne.

This is an excellent plain receipt for stewing a hare; but the dish may be enriched with forcemeat rolled into small balls, and simmered for ten minutes in the stew, or fried and added to it after it is dished; a higher seasoning of spice, a couple of glasses of port wine, with a little additional thickening and a tablespoon of lemon-juice, will all serve to give it a heightened relish.'

For the forcemeat balls:
'Take 2 small rashers of bacon, chopped, and fry with a small chopped onion in a tiny bit of butter until golden. Mix with 1 tbsp suet, 4 tbsp fresh white breadcrumbs, 1 tbsp chopped parsley, a bit of chopped thyme and sage, grated rind of ½ a lemon, salt and pepper and a trickle of beaten egg. Form into walnut-sized balls, roll in flour, dip into beaten egg and roll in more breadcrumbs. Fry until golden in dripping or oil.'

Pigeon with Peas   serves 4

Peas stewed with pigeon is a classic of French bourgeois cooking. It is even very, very good when cooked with fine quality tinned French petits pois rather than garden fresh or frozen. In fact, the latter are often far too sweet. A little optional shredded lettuce added to the pot towards the end of the cooking can be a welcome textural contrast.

4 French pigeons or squabs
a little softened butter
Maldon sea salt and freshly ground
   black pepper
4–5 slices of smoked pancetta *or*
   streaky bacon, cut into strips
approx. 20 small shallots, peeled

1 small glass dry white wine
2 small cans or 1 large can of French
   petits pois, drained and rinsed
   (look for the description on the
   can – 'à l'etuvée')
3–4 sprigs tarragon

Preheat the oven to 425°F/220°C/gas mark 7.
   Put the pigeons or squabs in a roasting dish, smear with the butter and

season. Roast for 10 minutes, basting a couple of times. Remove from the oven, tip off the fat into a cast-iron casserole pot and put the birds aside to cool. Turn the oven down to 300°F/150°C/gas mark 2.

Gently cook the *pancetta* or bacon and the shallots in the decanted fat until well gilded. Add the wine and reduce by half. Tip in the peas and bury the pigeons in them. Add a little more butter to the pigeon breasts if you like. Submerge the tarragon too. Simmer gently on top of the stove for a few minutes, until you are sure things are quite hot. Then put a lid on and place in the oven for 30 minutes. Serve directly from the pot. I don't think you need to eat anything else with this.

Offal

Genoese Tripe Soup ‡ serves 4, generously

Colman Andrews' astonishingly fine book on the cooking of the Riviera, *Flavors of the Riviera: Discovering Real Mediterranean Cooking*, has been my most recent favourite reading matter, gastronomically speaking. It is published by Bantam Books (USA), but has not yet been published here. I bought mine in America, but Books for Cooks (0171 221 1992) in London have surely done their very best to import some copies.

By 'Riviera' he means the section of coast (although he discusses the importance of their respective hinterlands too) that runs from Nice (Alpes Maritimes), in France, right the way down to La Spezia (still just within Liguria). Genoa, the capital, lies on the coast about two-thirds of the way, and is possibly more famous for *pesto alla Genovese* than anything else at all. This recipe for Genoese Tripe Soup (Sbïra) really caught my eye.

Note: In the original recipe, it is suggested that the tripe is previously blanched in boiling water for 30 seconds with some vinegar. However, tripe that is sold on these shores is already very well blanched indeed – too much, actually. This already diminishes the flavour, so to do it once more seems pointless. The taste of vinegar, however, should not be overlooked when preparing tripe. So might I suggest that a trickle of fine red wine vinegar is introduced towards the end of the cooking time. It will bring the whole dish together.

100g butter

a splash of olive oil

3–4 flat-leaf parsley sprigs, finely chopped

3–4 sprigs thyme, leaves only

3–4 sprigs of marjoram or oregano, leaves only

100g veal bone marrow (ask your butcher to saw enough marrow bones into 5cm pieces, soak them in cold water and scoop out the marrow; a couple of large bones should suffice)

4 level tbsp tomato paste

2 litres well-flavoured beef stock

1 kg honeycomb (if possible) beef tripe, cut into pieces about 5cm × 3cm

1kg waxy potatoes, peeled and cut into 1.5cm slices

Maldon sea salt and freshly ground white pepper

4 large thick slices of country style bread, toasted

freshly grated Parmesan cheese

Melt the butter with the olive oil in a suitable pot over low heat, then add the parsley, thyme, marjoram or oregano, and marrow, and cook together, stirring as the marrow melts, for about 5 minutes. Add the tomato paste and half the beef stock, stirring well so that the tomato paste melts into the mixture.

Add the tripe, cover the pot, and cook over a very low heat for 2½ hours. Add the remaining beef stock and the potatoes and season to taste. Continue cooking, covered, for 40 minutes.

To serve, place one piece of toast in each of four large shallow bowls and ladle tripe and broth over it. Serve with Parmesan, to be stirred in by each diner according to taste.

Rognons de Veau à la Moutarde ⚜ serves 4

In winter, at the famous Parisian brasserie La Coupole, I like to eat a lot of oysters followed by *rognons à la moutarde* (veal kidneys in a smashing mustard cream sauce) and finish with a *parfait au café*. What is always finally a pity for me is that I am none too keen on their magisterial *choucroute garni*, that steaming pile of sausages, cabbage and salted belly pork loved by almost every Parisian. So here is my version of those delicious creamed kidneys, another archetypal brasserie favourite.

Veal kidneys can be difficult to come by, so substitute lamb's if you need to, but make sure whichever you use is super-fresh.

2 small veal kidneys or 12 lamb's kidneys, divested of all suet and excess sinew
1 tbsp olive oil
25g butter
2 large shallots, thinly sliced
3 tbsp medium sherry
75ml dry white wine

1 heaped tbsp best Dijon mustard
150ml double cream
1 small clove of garlic, crushed to a paste
a few leaves of tarragon, chopped
Maldon sea salt and freshly ground black pepper
a squeeze of lemon juice

If using veal kidneys, separate the lobes with a small knife at their natural divisions and slice in half. If using lamb's, then simply cut into 4–5 slices along their length.

Heat the olive oil until smoking in a roomy frying pan. Briskly fry the kidneys until lightly coloured all over and stiffened from the heat; do not crowd the pan and do it in two batches if necessary. Tip into a sieve suspended over a bowl. Melt the butter in the pan and gently stew the shallots until well softened and golden. Pour in the sherry and wine and reduce until syrupy. Add the mustard, cream, garlic and tarragon. Simmer until rich and unctuous. Reheat the kidneys in this for one to two minutes, check the seasoning, stir in the lemon juice and serve with plain boiled potatoes.

Note: You will notice that some blood has dripped into the bowl that was under the kidneys. Do not add to the dish as it will coagulate the sauce.

Black Pudding with Colcannon and Parsley Sauce ‡ serves 4

It does not really matter whether you use black pudding or *boudin noir* for this dish. It depends on how rich you want the dish to be, noting that the Continental *boudin noir* is much the richer of the two. The parsley sauce is wonderfully simple by the way, but you will need a blender for the best results.

Champ is one of two favourite ways with mashed potatoes in the Irish Republic; the other is colcannon, where cabbage is added to buttery mashed potato, rather than the spring onions used here. Having said that, the cabbage mash would be equally good.

5 medium potatoes, peeled and cut into chunks
200g butter
6 spring onions, trimmed and finely chopped

Maldon sea salt and freshly ground black pepper
1 large bunch flat-leaf parsley, leaves only
250ml whipping cream
4 black puddings

Boil the potatoes in salted water, mash, and mix with half the butter, the spring onions and the seasoning. Keep hot, covered, in a low oven.

Tip the parsley into another pan of boiling water, cook for 2 minutes, drain in a colander and rinse thoroughly under very cold water. Squeeze dry in a tea towel. Boil together the remaining butter, the cream and the seasoning and put into a blender with the parsley. Purée until smooth and bright green. Do not over-blend for fear of splitting the sauce and always make sure the cream and butter are really hot.

Keep the sauce warm while you fry, steam, bake or grill your chosen pudding.

Serve the pudding, mash and sauce in the configuration that most pleases you.

Chicken Liver Pilaf ⁛ serves 4

With so many restaurants recently – from the highly luxurious to the good-yet-humble – opting to cook either foie gras or calf's liver as their choice of that particular offal, it has occurred to me that the simple chicken liver has been a little forgotten of late. It seems that its only regular appearance is either in a warm salad, with croutons, frisée leaves, bacon and a punchy mustard dressing (at least that is how it ought to be) or whizzed into the ubiquitous parfait of chicken livers that these days always seems to include foie gras, too, as a matter of course.

It is good to cook this savoury pilaf in the pot you will serve it in; from stove top to oven and then finally to table (a lidded Le Creuset, or similar, will be ideal). I don't think it necessary to serve anything else with this substantial supper dish.

1 tbsp olive oil
400g fresh chicken livers, trimmed
of all raggedy bits, but left
whole
50g butter

1 large onion, peeled and finely
chopped
2 cloves garlic, peeled and sliced
300g basmati rice, washed thoroughly
and drained well

4 cloves
4 cardamom pods
½ stick cinnamon
¼ tsp dried chilli flakes
½ tsp saffron threads
450 ml chicken stock

1 tbsp currants
4 pieces lemon rind
Maldon sea salt and freshly ground
   black pepper
2 tbsp coarsely chopped flat-leaf
   parsley

Preheat the oven to 375°F/190°C/gas mark 5.

Heat the olive oil in the pot until smoking. Add the chicken livers in a single layer and briefly fry on each side for seconds only; they must still be raw inside. Lift out and put to cool on a plate. Add the butter to the pot and fry the onion and garlic until golden. Tip in the rice and gently stew for a couple of minutes, stirring constantly until the rice glistens with the butter. Add the cloves, cardamom, cinnamon, chilli and saffron and stir in too. Pour in the stock and bring up to a simmer. Tip in the currants and lemon rind, taste the liquid and then season. Simmer very gently until the mixture starts to become more of a slurry. Now put in the chicken livers and carefully bury them underneath the rice. Switch off the heat, put the lid on and place in the oven. Remove from the oven after 20 minutes, but don't take off the lid for a further 10 minutes (this allows the rice to finish cooking). Gently fluff up the rice with a fork and spoon, mixing in the parsley as you go. Serve directly.

Chicken Livers in Peppercorn Jelly ‡

serves 4–5

Try not to be put off doing this recipe just because you have to make this jelly thing, as all it is, in essence, is a chicken stock that has been set with the gelatine that exudes from some pig's trotters as they cook. And if any is left over, it can only be a good thing. The result, as you can see from the photograph, is a joy to behold and just as impressive to eat.

For the jelly:
500g chicken wings
1 pig's trotter, split lengthways by the butcher
1 litre water
275ml dry white wine
1 onion, peeled and chopped
1 carrot, peeled and chopped
2 sticks celery, chopped
3 cloves
3–4 thyme sprigs
2 bay leaves
½ chicken stock cube
350g beautiful fresh chicken livers, cleaned of all green stains and sinewy bits

For the clarification:
200g raw, skinless chicken meat, chopped
110g trimmed and cleaned chicken livers
2 large egg whites
1 onion, peeled and chopped
1 carrot, peeled and chopped
4–5 sprigs parsley
75ml Madeira or medium sherry
1 tbsp sherry vinegar

To finish:
1 tsp white peppercorns and 1 tsp black peppercorns, coarsely crushed and sieved to remove excess pepper powder

Put all the ingredients for the jelly in a large pan and bring gently up to the boil, removing any scum as it forms. Cook at the gentlest simmer for 2 hours. Drain in a large colander set over another large pan. Lift out the pieces of chicken and the trotters and either discard, or – I would strongly suggest – pick the shreds of meat off them, chop them to a paste (don't use a food processor, *please*) and use to make some delicious potted meat, moistened with a little of the stock so that they set. Season with nutmeg, cayenne and mace, and cover with melted butter to seal. This is *real* cooking.

Once the stock has settled after draining, lift off any fat from the surface with several sheets of kitchen paper. Take a few ladles of the stock and put into a separate pan. Bring to a simmer and poach the chicken livers gently for no more than a couple of minutes; the texture of the livers should be bouncy, but not firm. Lift out and allow to cool completely on a plate. Return this small amount of liver-poaching stock to the original.

Put all the ingredients for the clarification into the bowl of a food processor. Work to a purée and mix into the cooled stock, preferably with your hands, mulching the clarification thoroughly into the liquid. Set onto a low heat and allow to come up to a simmer very slowly. When the first signs of froth and scum appear, and the clarification mush is starting to solidify, a trickle of the stock will come up through the mess. Allow this to happen in various places and then turn off the heat. Leave for a few minutes and then repeat the process twice more. Now set onto the lowest possible flame and leave to percolate for 40 minutes. Switch off the heat and leave to settle for 10 minutes.

Wet a scrupulously clean (though not perfumed with Lenor or Comfort) tea towel or muslin and use it to line a sieve. Suspend over a roomy bowl or pan. Now, using a slotted spoon, remove a portion of the mulchy meat raft from the surface and discard. Take a ladle, and through the hole you have made – which resembles a perforation in a frozen lake – transfer the now clarified stock from underneath into the lined sieve. Allow to drip through, but under no circumstances consider pressing any solid matter that might collect, as this will cloud the jelly.

Set the clear jelly in a bowl set over another one filled with ice. Stirring from time to time, allow the jelly to become syrupy. Once this starts to happen, lift the jelly from the ice and stir in the peppercorns. Cut the poached and cooled chicken livers into dice and put into small ramekins or one larger shallow dish. Spoon over the jelly to completely cover the livers and put into the fridge to set for at least 3 hours. Serve in the pots or spooned out of the single dish with a warmed spoon. Crisp buttered toast and *cornichons* would make suitable accompaniments.

Pieds de Cochon Sainte Menehould ⸸

serves 4

Many recipes that I have read for the initial cooking of trotters – i.e., before they are turned into actual 'dishes' – give no indication whatsoever of the transformation that takes place over this period. They turn into a twisted mutant shape if left as they are, so they need to be tethered.

The best thing to use is a small piece of wood (clingfilmed and then wrapped in foil), roughly the shape of a trotter, and flat. Tie each trotter securely in three or four places to its piece of wood and put into a deep dish that will take them tightly. This method will ensure a more recognizable trotter, once cooked.

The French term *à la Sainte Menehould* (a small town near Bar-le-Duc) refers to various fatty and gelatinous cuts that are breadcrumbed and then grilled or baked, resulting in a crusted surface. One of the very best examples is the one that uses breast of lamb (a much underrated cut), a recipe for which can be found in *An Omelette and a Glass of Wine* by Elizabeth David.

2 carrots, peeled and sliced
1 large onion, peeled and sliced
3 sticks celery
4 cloves
2 bay leaves
3–4 sprigs thyme
Maldon sea salt and a few
    peppercorns
4 pig's trotters, singed of any surface
    hair with a blowtorch or over a gas
    flame, then well rinsed
1–2 tbsp plain flour
2 small eggs, beaten
1 tbsp Dijon mustard
4 tbsp fresh white breadcrumbs
melted butter

For the Sauce Gribiche:
1 tbsp smooth Dijon mustard
2 tbsp tarragon vinegar
Maldon sea salt and freshly ground
    black pepper
275–325 ml groundnut or other
    flavourless oil
1½ tbsp capers, drained, squeezed dry
    and coarsely chopped
5 sprigs tarragon, leaves only, finely
    chopped
5 hard-boiled egg yolks, sieved

Preheat the oven to 275°F/130°C/gas mark 1.

Distribute the vegetables, herbs and seasoning in and around the trotters. Just cover with water, bring up to a simmer, skim off any resultant scum, cover and braise in the oven for 1½–2 hours. Test with a small sharp knife here and there for tenderness (this can be confusing considering the amount of bones); they should feel a bit floppy.

Carefully lift out the trotters, flicking off any clinging bits of veg, and put onto a plate to cool completely. Strain the liquor into a bowl – this can be used for savoury jellies or as an enricher for gravies and sauces.

Preheat the oven to 425°F/220°C/gas mark 7; also an overhead grill.

Once the trotters are cold and stiff, take a serrated knife and cut in half lengthways, with the knife running through the cloven hoof (the bones will now be soft and should not offer any resistance to the knife, and this is also the most natural divide through the foot). Lay the eight halves out onto a plate. Season lightly and then dust each one with the flour. Mix together the eggs and mustard and brush this liberally over each trotter. Roll in the breadcrumbs and put onto a wire rack. Place this onto a large baking tray and trickle over a little of the melted butter. Bake in the oven for about 15 minutes and then finish off under the grill if necessary, so that all are crusted and golden.

To make the Sauce Gribiche, liquidize or whisk together the mustard, vinegar and seasoning. With the motor still running (or still whisking), start pouring in the oil in a thin stream. When you have used about three-quarters of the oil, switch off and taste for acidity and seasoning. The mixture should have started to thicken somewhat and may need thinning down with some lukewarm water; the desired thickness of the finished sauce should be similar to bottled salad cream. Continue adding more oil if necessary and also some water perhaps. When this basic dressing is complete, stir in the capers, tarragon and egg yolks. Serve with the piping hot trotters.

Note: If you wish to serve the trotters as *Pieds de Cochon Vinaigrette* – the classic of all respectable French *charcuteries* – then simply put the split trotters (un-breaded) directly into a deep serving dish, cut side up, and spoon over only the basic dressing. Sprinkle with parsley and finely chopped onion. Serve with a pot of *cornichons* on the side.

Warm Chicken Liver Mousses ‡ serves 6

This is a classic of the rich cookery of the Lyonnais. One of the most famous renditions of that gastronomic region is to serve it with an equally rich crayfish cream sauce, which, strange as it may sound, works wonderfully. As fresh live crayfish are not readily available at your local supermarket or fishmonger, try it with your favourite tomato sauce, liquidized to a luxurious smoothness with a little butter and cream, and not, for once, with olive oil please.

The 100g of bone marrow in the recipe should be obtainable from two veal bones and sliced by the butcher on his handy bandsaw. When you get the pieces home, soak the bones in cold water in the sink, for an hour or so. This will help loosen the marrow, so that it may be eased out with the fingers.

*100g bone marrow, chopped into
  chunks*
150ml milk
150ml single cream
*1 clove garlic, peel and green germ
  removed, coarsely chopped*
1 small shallot, peeled and chopped

2 eggs
1 egg yolk
*150g chicken livers, trimmed of all
  sinew and any green parts*
¼ tsp salt
freshly ground white pepper
freshly grated nutmeg

Put the bone marrow, milk, cream, garlic and shallot into a small pan and heat to only just warm; this will soften the bone marrow. Leave to cool to room temperature. Put the remaining ingredients into the liquidizer and purée. Once the milk/bone marrow mixture has cooled, add the puréed livers and blend all together until really smooth. Pass through a fine sieve into a bowl and leave to settle for 10 minutes.

Place a steamer on to heat up (this is undoubtedly the best way to cook these little mousses) and also generously butter 6 small ramekins or dariole moulds; a small disc of greaseproof paper placed in the base of each will also ease removal of the mousses once cooked.

Now that the mousse mixture has settled, remove the scum that has collected on the surface with a small ladle. Stir the mixture gently and ladle into the prepared moulds. Cover each one with a piece of foil and place into the steamer. Turn the heat down and simmer for 10 minutes. Now, without removing the lid, leave the mousses to finish cooking in the residual heat for a further 40 minutes. Lift off the foil, carefully run a small knife around the inside of the moulds and turn out onto hot plates. Spoon over the tomato sauce and serve.

Vegetable Dishes

Courgette Terrine   ‡   serves 4–6

If there is one dish of the last fifteen years or so that gives me the willies, it is the vegetable terrine. I know I am not alone in this hatred of, let's face it, a fairly harmless dish. I just can't see the point of it, that's all; those little bits of vegetable set into a chicken (or ham) mousse. I mean, it's not even fit for veggies, is it? But there have been some shockers, sitting in their pool of lurid tomato coulis. Sadly, it became a dish you just 'had to have been seen to have a go at'.

Anyway, this charming little courgette thingy is not like that at all. It's all harmonious: eggs, a little cream, a pertinent herb and the courgettes themselves. And if you must serve it with a tomato coulis, then you can jolly well look elsewhere for a recipe. Incidentally the recipe was given to me by my nice neighbour, Suzanne.

1 kg very fresh and firm courgettes, trimmed	freshly ground white pepper
1 level tsp salt	4 small eggs
50g butter	250 ml double cream
	1 level tbsp chopped dill or tarragon

Coarsely grate the courgettes. Mix with the salt and put in a colander. Leave to drain for 1 hour. Squeeze dry in a tea towel until no more excess juice drips out. Preheat the oven to 325°F/160°C/gas mark 3. Melt the butter in a roomy frying pan (preferably non-stick) and gently cook the courgettes for 5–10 minutes with some pepper. Do not allow to colour. Tip onto a plate and cool. Thoroughly mix together the eggs, cream and chosen herb, but do not whisk too much: if the custard is too light and airy, it will only sink back after cooking and cooling. Stir the courgettes into the custard and check the seasoning. Pour the mixture into a 1 litre loaf tin (again, preferably non-stick), the base lined with a sheet of greaseproof paper. Put into a roasting tin filled with enough water to come at least three-quarters of the way up the sides of the loaf tin. Cover with foil and cook for about 1–1½ hours. Check from time to time; the terrine is ready when it feels firm to the touch and a bit bouncy. Remove from the water and leave to cool for 10 minutes before carefully turning out. Cool completely, then chill in the fridge. Slice, and serve with a judiciously dressed tomato salad, or a freshly made, not too spicy, Mexican style tomato salsa.

Courgettes en Persillade ‡ serves 4

I made this for lunch once, whilst staying with friends in Provence. I had already purchased the courgettes, because they looked good in the market – the only reason to buy *anything*. I already had some parsley, breadcrumbs, garlic, lemon and Parmesan – and there was always olive oil lurking. The dish took only a few minutes to prepare, plus a bit of time for the salting. 'Persillade', in Provence, refers to anything cooked with parsley and garlic, and most usually with breadcrumbs too, to soak up any oil and then turn deliciously crisp and golden.

1 kg large courgettes, peeled, deseeded and cut into 1.5cm chunks
a little Maldon sea salt

For the *persillade*:
50g chunk of stale white bread, torn into pieces
2 cloves garlic, peeled and chopped

1 small bunch flat-leaf parsley, leaves only
grated rind of ½ a lemon
very little Maldon sea salt and freshly ground black pepper
3–4 tbsp olive oil
lemon wedges
freshly grated Parmesan (optional)

Preheat the oven to 475°F/250°C/gas mark 9.

Lightly salt the courgettes and put into a colander to drain for 30 minutes. Rinse them briefly and dry thoroughly in a clean tea towel. Make the *persillade* by putting all the ingredients into a food processor. Chop briefly, until the ingredients look like pale green breadcrumbs, but do not overwork as the mixture may become doughy.

Now heat 2–3 tbsp of the olive oil in a roomy frying pan until very hot, and quickly fry the courgettes so that they take on a little colour, but not at all cooked. Tip into an attractive shallow oven-to-table dish. Strew

129

generously with the *persillade* and drizzle over a little extra olive oil. Put into the oven on the top shelf and bake for about 10 minutes until the crust is crisp and golden. Serve straightaway with the wedges of lemon to squeeze over each serving and a little grated Parmesan if you feel like it.

This is a perfect dish for a light lunch, on its own, with nothing else. Well . . . perhaps a glass of cool Provençal rosé might not go amiss.

Leeks and Potatoes Baked with Anchovies ⁑ serves 4

Leeks and potatoes were just waiting to get married. But who knows who was responsible for their nuptials? However, I might hazard a guess that Parmentier might well have introduced the happy couple.

For it was this Frenchman, one Antoine Parmentier, who introduced the potato to his country during the reign of Louis XVI. Having returned from the Seven Years War, when he was fed on potatoes as a prisoner of the Prussians, he apparently presented Marie Antoinette with a bouquet of potato flowers. So impressed was she by them, she promptly decorated her hair with one, assuring Parmentier a name in French gastronomic history books.

This is the sort of dish you might want for a light lunch or late supper.

4 large fat leeks, trimmed, cut into
   2.5 cm circles and carefully washed
   so as to keep the shape intact
a little softened butter
about 12–14 small waxy potatoes,
   boiled in their skins until half
   cooked, peeled and sliced in half
   lengthways

1 clove garlic, peeled and finely
   chopped
1 x 50g tin anchovy fillets, chopped
150 ml whipping cream
150 ml milk
½ tbsp snipped chives
freshly ground black pepper
Maldon sea salt

Preheat the oven to 375°F/°190C/gas mark 5.

Briefly boil the leeks until still a little crunchy. Drain well for at least

Left: Courgettes en Persillade

131

Vegetable Dishes

10 minutes. Lightly butter an ovenproof dish and distribute the leeks and potatoes in a random fashion. In a bowl, mix together the garlic, anchovies, cream and milk, and then carefully spoon over the leeks. Put in the oven and bake for 30 minutes until the top is pale golden, the cream/milk mixture has thickened considerably and the vegetables are cooked through; check with a skewer or small knife. Strew with the chives and grind over plenty of pepper. The anchovies should have provided the dish with enough saline content, but if not, sprinkle over a little flaked Maldon sea salt.

Warm Leek Purée with Truffle Oil ‡

serves 4

This is an exceptionally easy dish, for one so luxurious. Although it is nothing more than a rather thick, ultra-smooth vichyssoise, its voluptuous qualities are further enhanced by the addition of the now ubiquitous white truffle oil. It seems that young chefs cannot put together a menu nowadays without a slick or two of it being administered over all sorts of preparations. I mean, it's OK now and again, but along with balsamic vinegar, shaved Parmesan, sun-dried tomatoes et al. (often all together, egad!), there does seem to be a plaguelike problem here. Anyway, it seems to work particularly well in this dish. Of course, if you happen to have to hand some fresh white truffles, then of course use these – but not both, please!

4 large fat leeks, all traces of green removed, thickly sliced and washed
1 large potato, peeled and cut into chunks
150 ml water

50 ml extra-virgin olive oil
Maldon sea salt and freshly ground white pepper
4 dsp double cream, warmed
1–2 tbsp truffle oil

Put the leeks, potato, water, olive oil and seasoning in a small heavy-bottomed saucepan. Bring up to a simmer and cook very gently indeed, or in a very low oven, until the vegetables are completely collapsed.

Whilst still hot (a cold mixture, when puréed, can become gluey) tip into a liquidizer and purée until very smooth and pass through a fine sieve. Serve warm, in shallow soup plates, with a little cream spooned over, and then anoint each with some of the truffle oil. Eat completely on its own. Any distraction such as crusty bread or croutons will spoil the sublime texture.

Baked Aubergines with Tomato, Onions, Garlic and Olive Oil ‡ serves 4

In my many years in the restaurant trade, I have found it to be the case that a small minority of vegetarian folk, radical in their beliefs, are often those that it seems fail to appreciate dishes on the menu that are specifically made with vegetables in mind rather than them; the dish prepared simply as something good to eat. It has not, how shall one say, been fashioned with a 'theme' in mind. Moreover, it has been cooked or assembled because it is a good idea. The following story is not a dig, but a happy and amusing tale of restaurant life.

Several years ago now, the personable, steadfast and upright Mr Graham Williams (then maître d', now head honcho of Bibendum) took the order of a particular American lady who was, it transpired, a vegan. G.W. went through the whole card with her, explaining all the dishes so she would know what she could, and could not, eat. The lady finally went for the Piedmontese peppers – roasted red peppers with tomato, olive oil, garlic and anchovies. Quite correctly, and with deference, she asked that the peppers might be unadorned by the anchovy fillets. 'Of course, madam,' the charming G.W. replied.

So off he sped into the kitchen to dispatch the order, where, promptly, the dish was swiftly assembled, complete with salty little brown slivers, and placed before the vegan from Virginia (or was it Vegas?). 'Forgive, forgive,' muttered G.W., suddenly seeing the offending anchovies just that brief moment too late.

Back in the kitchen. 'I told you not to put bloody anchovies on it! Why

can't you just listen for once!' he bawled quite rightly at the cold first courses chef, or some similar words to that effect . . . So we picked off the fishy bits and sent the plate back out to the dining room.

'Erm . . . did you, by any chance, just remove the anchovies and give it back to me?' the lady asked. 'Erm . . . yes, we did do just that,' G.W. whimpered, honestly. 'Well, I'm sorry, but I can't eat it. I'll have the risotto with white truffles instead' – one of the other possible vegetarian choices on our lengthy menu of international cuisine. 'But, madam,' G.W. shrieked, 'you can't possibly have that! The truffles have been on the end of a pig's nose!'

Here is a really nice little vegetable dish for everyone to enjoy.

2 medium onions, peeled and sliced	Maldon sea salt and freshly ground
4 cloves garlic, peeled and sliced	black pepper
4 small aubergines, with stalks	10–12 basil leaves, torn into pieces
8 ripe small tomatoes	a generous splash of dry white
6 tbsp olive oil	wine

Preheat the oven to 350°F/180°C/gas mark 4.

Mix the onions with the garlic and scrunch together with your hands in a large bowl. Set aside. Cut the aubergines in half lengthways, slicing right through the stalk as well. Then, starting to cut from just below the stalk and continuing towards the bulbous end and right through, slice the halves lengthways in four or five neat cuts, thus creating a sort of fan effect. Remove the cores of the tomatoes, cut them in half vertically, cut them into thickish slices and then cut each one to make a half-circle. Now, on a work surface, sit each aubergine half cut-side down. In each of the aubergine gaps, push the tomato half-circles (rounded side up) up towards the stalk until all the tomato pieces have been exhausted. You should now have eight halves of aubergine with three lines of red tomato slices poking out of each.

Smear 2 tbsp of the olive oil into the bottom of an ovenproof dish, pile in half the onion and garlic mixture and spread out flat. Add a little seasoning and half the basil. With the help of a fish slice or similar, carefully place the aubergines on top, skin side up, being careful not to let the

Left: **Baked Aubergines with Tomato, Onions, Garlic and Olive Oil**

tomatoes fall out. Sprinkle over the rest of the basil and spread over the remaining onion and garlic mixture. Give the dish a final seasoning, spoon over the remaining olive oil and douse with the white wine. Cover with foil and bake in the oven for 40 minutes to 1 hour, or until the aubergines are very soft and the onions have completely wilted. Serve at room temperature with good bread.

Hot Beetroot Purée   serves 4

In his seminal work, *Cuisine Gourmande*, the brilliant French chef Michel Guérard gives a recipe for a hot sweet and sour purée of beetroot and tomato that he suggests serving with game; of which, personally, I might choose a roasted saddle of hare as being the ideal vehicle.

100g tomatoes
1 tsp olive oil
150g onions, peeled and thinly
   sliced
1 clove garlic, peeled and crushed
3 tbsp red wine vinegar (or sherry
   vinegar, which lends a particularly
   interesting note)

350g cooked beetroot, peeled and
   thinly sliced
Maldon sea salt and freshly ground
   black pepper
1 tbsp double cream
scant 150ml good hot chicken stock
   (home-made preferably, or use a
   cube at a pinch)

Plunge the tomatoes into boiling water for 10 seconds, drain and slip off their skins. Slice in two and squeeze out the pips in your hands. Coarsely chop the flesh, put onto a plate and set aside. Heat the olive oil in a saucepan, and in it gently fry the onions and garlic until soft but not coloured. Pour in the vinegar, and add the tomato pulp and beetroot. Season, partially cover and cook over a very low light for 1 hour (use one of those heat-diffuser pads if you have one).

Once cooked, purée in a liquidizer, together with the cream and stock (you may not need all the stock) until the mixture is very smooth and light in texture. You may prefer to use a food processor for this, but the purée may not become as smooth as it might in a liquidizer. Keep warm, covered, in a bowl suspended over barely simmering water, until needed.

Cold Beetroot Purée or *Chrain*

serves 6–8 as a relish

I used to do a really wicked thing within the privacy of the kitchens at Bibendum. Come Sunday morning, when the final grindings of fresh horseradish root to accompany roast beef for lunch were underway, I would alert an unsuspecting waiter on one of his various treks past my station.

'Good morning, Gavin! How are you? Smell this! It's wonderful!' Trusting Gavin (silly Gavin) would thrust his nose into the goblet of the liquidizer and inhale deeply. 'Mmmm . . . lovely,' he would automatically say, swiftly followed by 'Oh, ****!!!' as the coughing fits started, the eyes watered, the face reddened. He would rush out of the kitchen with a bewildered expression, not to say shocked. New chefs had already received the same initiation early on in their sojourn, so they felt ready to mark the waiter's retreating stagger with much audible mirth and merriment. Oh! the joys of the restaurant kitchen. Just like school.

Horseradish puréed with cooked beetroot is – as far as I know – called *chrain*. In Jewish delis that I know and occasionally frequent, it is particularly good smeared onto deliciously greasy *latkes*. The fume reaction that occurs when the deep purple beetroot meshes with the snowy white horseradish is even more sensationally spectacular than the horseradish alone. Lethal indeed. So go search out a particularly loathsome noisy neighbour.

4–5 medium sized cooked beetroots, peeled and cut into chunks
1 × 175g piece of fresh horseradish root, peeled and freshly grated

1 tbsp balsamic vinegar
2 level tbsp caster sugar
Maldon sea salt to taste

Simply blend all the ingredients in a food processor until coarsely puréed. It will keep in the fridge, in a screw-top jar, for a couple of weeks.

Mushrooms on Toast   ‡   serves 4

This is a luxuriously rich dish, and quite expensive to make. The mushrooms to use are dried morels (the expensive bit), which are now fairly easy to come across in good supermarkets and delicatessens. Other dried mushrooms may be substituted, but morels are best, as their crenellated surface catches and holds the rich cream sauce in the most agreeable way.

25g dried morels
400ml warm water
4 small shallots, peeled and finely
   chopped
50g butter
1 clove garlic, peeled and finely
   chopped
1 small glass Madeira or medium
   sherry

275ml double cream
Maldon sea salt and freshly ground
   black pepper
juice of ½ a small lemon
a little chopped tarragon or chervil, and
   some chives
4 thickish slices bread, toasted and
   buttered

Soak the morels in the water for about 30 minutes. Drain (reserve the liquid), squeeze the mushrooms dry in your hands and strain the liquid through a fine sieve into a small pan. Reduce it over a gentle heat until it measures no more than about 3–4 tbsp. Whilst this is going on, fry the shallots in the butter until pale golden and stir in the garlic. Add the morels and cook gently for five minutes, stirring frequently. Add the Madeira or sherry, bring up to a simmer and stew for a good 10 minutes, until the mixture is starting to dry out. Add the reduced soaking water and the cream. Bring up to a simmer once more and continue cooking until the whole mass is creamy and unctuous. Season and stir in the lemon juice and herbs. Leave to gently bubble away while you make the toast. Pile the

Right: **Mushrooms on Toast**

creamed morels onto the buttered toast and serve without delay. A chilled glass of fino goes particularly well with this.

Beetroots in Parsley Sauce ‡ serves 4

There are a few dedicated cooks who know about beetroots with parsley sauce and how to make a nice bortsch, for instance, neither of which require a great deal of toil and trouble to make. Joyce Molyneux, of the much celebrated Carved Angel in Dartmouth, serves a truly delicious hot dish of grated beetroot with hot salted ox-tongue, to great effect. Anyway, here is the parsley sauce combo. Do not leave the sauce with the beetroots for too long before serving, as they bleed horribly quickly.

16 (approx.) small raw beetroots; usually sold in bunches, similar to small turnips
Maldon sea salt

For the parsley sauce:
1 healthy bunch of flat-leaf parsley
500ml milk
1 small onion, peeled and chopped
3 pieces of pithless lemon zest

2 cloves
1 sprig thyme
1 bay leaf
50g butter
50g plain flour
100ml double cream
freshly grated nutmeg
Maldon sea salt and freshly ground black pepper

Wash the beets well, snip off their trailing roots and tops, put into a pan and cover with water. Add a little salt and bring up to the boil. Simmer, uncovered, until the beets are tender when pierced with a small knife – about 40 minutes or thereabouts. Meanwhile, make the parsley sauce.

Pick the leaves off the bunch of parsley and set aside. Coarsely chop up the stalks and put into a saucepan. Add the milk, onion, lemon zest, cloves, thyme and bay leaf. Heat together and bring up to a simmer. Cook very gently for 5 minutes, switch off the heat, put a lid on, and leave to infuse for 30 minutes.

By now the beets should be cooked. Drain them, peel whilst still warm – the simplest of tasks as the skins just slip away in your fingers – and put into a serving dish. Cover with foil and keep hot in a low oven.

Melt the butter in another pan (preferably with a thick base) and stir in the flour to make a roux. Strain the flavoured milk onto this, stirring constantly, and once more bring up to a simmer, using a heat-diffuser pad if you have one. Set the pan onto this and allow to cook ever so gently over a thread of heat for about 10 minutes. Chop the parsley leaves very finely and add to the sauce together with the cream and nutmeg. Simmer for a further 5 minutes so that the parsley flavours the sauce, check for seasoning and pour over the hot beetroots. Serve at once. Very good with roast lamb and mint sauce for Sunday lunch.

Spinach and Ricotta Cakes with Mustard Sauce ‡ serves 4

This agreeable adaptation of a spinach gnocchi recipe can also be transformed into the most delicious fried cakes. Chopped spinach is mixed with fresh ricotta cheese, eggs, a little flour and Parmesan, formed into small cakes, dipped in flour, egg and breadcrumbs and fried in hot oil. Usually, gnocchi are poached or steamed, but here the mixture develops a gorgeous crusted coating, with all the creamy bits kept securely within.

750g spinach
75g fresh ricotta cheese
3 egg yolks
100g freshly grated Parmesan
Maldon sea salt and freshly ground
*   black pepper*
¼ of a whole nutmeg, grated
plain flour

1 egg, beaten
2–3 tbsp fresh white breadcrumbs
groundnut oil for frying

For the mustard sauce:
275ml double cream
2 tbsp Dijon mustard
3–4 dashes of Tabasco

Blanch the spinach in boiling water for a couple of minutes. Drain and refresh under very cold running water. Squeeze in a tea towel until completely dry. Note: it is most important that the squeezing of the spinach is thorough; the mixture is naturally soft, but any excess liquid will cause it to be unmanageable. Purée the spinach, ricotta, egg yolks, Parmesan, seasoning and nutmeg. Spread out onto a shallow tray, cover with clingfilm and put in the fridge to firm up, for at least 2 hours.

To form the cakes, first flour your hands. Take up the equivalent of 1 large tbsp of the mixture and form into a rounded cake. Place on a floured surface and neaten up into a flat sort of fishcake shape. Put onto a tray covered with clingfilm. Make seven more and, once more, put into the fridge to firm up.

Preheat the oven to 350°F/180°C/gas mark 4.

Gently roll the cakes in flour, then in egg and finally in the breadcrumbs. Heat about 4 tablespoonfuls of the oil in a large frying pan until hot but not smoking (if the pan can take all the cakes in one go, all the better; if not, cook in two batches of four). Gently place the cakes in the hot oil and fry for a couple of minutes on each side, until golden brown. Place on a rack, suspended on an oven tray, and place in the oven. Finish the cooking here for a further 15–20 minutes.

Meanwhile make this very easy mustard sauce. In a small saucepan, heat the cream and whisk in the mustard and Tabasco. Simmer for about 5 minutes until custardy-thick and unctuous.

Serve two cakes per person, on four hot plates, and pour the sauce over and around. Decorate with a few sprightly sprigs of watercress if you like.

Spinach with Chickpeas ‡

serves 8 as a tapa, or 4–5 as a soup

This recipe comes from one of my very favourite cookery books: *Traditional Spanish Cooking* by Janet Mendel. In Seville, she says, this is served as a tapa. The mixture turns out fairly sloppy, but is thicker than a soup. I recently – and with much success – turned it into more of a soup, by slightly increasing the given amount of water. To compensate for this, I also upped the quantity of garlic, spices and vinegar. I suggest you make it in the original way first; both out of respect for Janet Mendel's excellent recipe and also to see how the dish should really be.

4 tbsp olive oil
2 slices (50g) country bread
4 cloves garlic
1 tsp cumin seeds or ground cumin
10 black peppercorns
1 piece dried chilli pepper
1 tsp salt
1 tbsp paprika

1 tbsp wine vinegar (sherry vinegar would also be good here)
225 ml water
750g cooked chickpeas (if you use canned ones, drain and rinse them first)
275g cooked spinach (or frozen)

Heat the oil in a pan and fry the bread and 2 cloves of the garlic until golden. Remove with a slotted spoon. In a mortar or food processor, grind this fried bread and garlic with the cumin, peppercorns, chilli, salt and a splash of warm water. Reserve. Into the oil remaining in the pan, add the remaining 2 garlic cloves (chopped). Stir in the paprika and immediately add the vinegar, the 225 ml of water and the mixture from the mortar or food processor. Add the chickpeas and spinach. Simmer for 20 minutes. Serve lukewarm or at room temperature.

Leeks in White Sauce ‡ serves 4

I have always felt very fond indeed towards leeks. My earliest recollections are of them plainly boiled in not very much water, drained and then blanketed in a white sauce. It is a basic, very English way of mildly tarting up a vegetable and turning it into a vegetable 'dish'. But when this was served up at home, I always enjoyed it: wet, warm, soggy really, but memorably comforting. Although my mother might not have taken too much trouble over a simple white sauce (she had a teaching job to do and also two children to bring up), it certainly made the leeks more interesting than just plain boiled. But now, with cooking being the most important thing to me, I can spend time on that white sauce, that delicious, beloved béchamel.

600 ml milk
4 cloves
1 onion, peeled and chopped
1 bay leaf
Maldon sea salt
75 g butter
50 g plain flour
150 ml single cream

freshly grated nutmeg
freshly ground white pepper
8 large leeks, trimmed of almost all the
    green parts, sliced into 5 cm lengths
    and then washed
Lancashire cheese (optional)
breadcrumbs (optional)

Heat together the milk, cloves, onion, bay leaf and a little salt. Simmer for a few minutes, cover and allow the flavours to mingle for about 30 minutes. In another pan, melt the butter and stir in the flour. Make a roux and gently cook the butter and flour together for a minute or two, but on no account allow it to colour; it must stay pale. But it *is* important that the flour cooks. Strain the milk into the roux and vigorously whisk together until smooth (this always gets rid of any lumps). On the lowest possible heat (preferably with a heat-diffuser pad), set the sauce to cook. You may think that the sauce is very thick to begin with. However, as it cooks, the consistency will become silky and unctuous and, remember, there is some cream to add at the end. Do not cover the sauce, stir from time to time with a wooden spoon and cook for about 30 minutes. Add the cream, nutmeg and pepper, mix in thoroughly, check for salt and cook for a further 5 minutes. Strain again into a clean pan and put a lid on, as this helps to prevent a skin forming. Keep warm.

Preheat the oven to 375°F/190°C/gas mark 5.

Put the kettle on and put the leeks into a pan. When the water has boiled, pour over the leeks and add a little salt. Bring back to the boil and cook for between 5 and 10 minutes, depending upon how thick your leeks are; test with a small sharp knife for tenderness. You don't want crunchy leeks, but conversely neither do you want sloppy ones. Drain carefully in a colander for a good 10 minutes, to ensure that all the water has drained away. Lay into a shallow ovenproof dish and pour over the sauce. If you want cheesy leeks then strew with a little grated Lancashire (my preference) and then strew lightly with fresh breadcrumbs. Dot with butter and put into the oven for about 20 minutes, or until lightly golden and bubbling around the edges. If you don't want cheese or breadcrumbs, just do the butter.

Braised Fennel   serves 4

One of the finest dishes using fennel that I have yet eaten was cooked by the remarkable Lulu Peyraud. I first met her at the Domaine Tempier vineyard, in the wine region of Bandol, near Toulon, in the South of France, where her late husband, Lucien, together with the entire Peyraud/Tempier family, have been making the finest of all Bandol wine for many years.

I was fortunate enough to be taken there for lunch (twice) by friends Richard Olney and Jill Norman, some three or four years ago now. Oh, what wonderful food she cooked! So simple and unaffected were the dishes we devoured that it would be impossible to convey to you exactly how they tasted on those two magical occasions. The fennel, however, really sang out. The following recipe is how I felt it might have been made.

Use a cast-iron dish for this recipe if at all possible (Le Creuset is perfect).

2 tbsp olive oil

4 large fennel bulbs, trimmed of bruised
    parts and cut in half (keep a few
    feathery fronds to chop and sprin-
    kle over the finished dish)

25g butter

Maldon sea salt and freshly ground
    black pepper

1 tbsp Pernod

3 tbsp white wine

juice of 1 small lemon

Preheat the oven to 300°F/150°C/gas mark 2.

Put the cooking dish directly onto a flame and heat the olive oil. Put in the fennel cut-side down and fry gently until well coloured. Turn over and add the butter. Allow to froth and turn down the heat. Season and add the Pernod and wine. Spoon these juices over the fennel and then add the lemon juice. Allow to bubble gently, cover with foil (or a lid if you have one that fits tightly) and bake in the oven for 1–1½ hours, or until really soft and meltingly tender. Allow to cool a little before serving, as the flavour is improved by eating lukewarm. Scatter with the chopped fronds. This is a very good vegetable served with roast pork or veal.

250g rice
200g grated buffalo mozzarella
100g freshly grated Parmesan
1 bunch basil, leaves only, roughly torn

a handful of flat-leafed parsley, roughly
chopped
Maldon sea salt and freshly ground
black pepper

Boil the rice in twice its volume of water till just cooked. Drain well and put half of it into a heated serving bowl. Add the cheeses, herbs and some seasoning, then cover with the rest of the rice. Now stir well until stringy – two large forks seem to do the trick. Serve immediately onto hot plates.

Risi e Bisi ‡ serves 4

The recipe for this comes from Marcella Hazan's *Classic Italian Cookbook*. I have always followed this recipe exactly and it performs beautifully. Hazan says, '*Risi e Bisi* is not risotto with peas. It is a soup, although a very thick one.' She is, as usual, spot on here. I adore this dish.

half an onion, peeled and chopped
50g butter
1kg fresh peas (unshelled weight),
shelled
Maldon sea salt

1 litre light Chicken Broth (see page 2)
200g Arborio rice
2 tbsp chopped parsley
50g freshly grated Parmesan

Put the onion in a pan with the butter and fry over a medium heat until pale gold. Add the peas and salt and gently cook for 2 minutes, stirring frequently. Add 700ml of the broth, cover, and cook at a very moderate boil for 10 minutes. Add the rice, parsley and the remaining broth, stir, cover, and cook at a slow boil for 15 minutes, or until the rice is tender but *al dente* – firm to the bite. Stir from time to time while cooking, and taste and check for salt. Just prior to serving, add the cheese, mixing it into the soup.

Risotto with Shellfish   ‡   serves 4

Risotto seems more synonymous with Venice than anywhere else in Italy, save perhaps Milan. But a risotto combined with shellfish is Venetian to a T, the Veneto being rich in crustacea, clams, fish generally. There are spider crabs served in the *ristorantes* of this town that are desirably dressed with olive oil and lemon, and from crabs that have been so recently boiled the flesh may still be warm from the pot.

The most remarkable clam found in the Veneto is the *cappi lunghi*, the razor clam. These are slapped under a grill, slicked by olive oil and garlic until bouncy with heat and by virtue of that, wondrously juicy and sweet. *Cappi sante*, scallops, are given similar treatment. By the way, Ristorante 'Da Fiore' does the best *cappi lunghi* in Venice. (Note: we have plenty of razor clams on our beaches. Does anybody commercially collect them?)

Use whatever shellfish is best looking when you go out shopping. Or rather, when you see some good shellfish, buy it and then decide to make a risotto; being a caring cook, you will, naturally, always have some risotto rice in the kitchen cupboard. If the variety of shellfish that you decide upon is not shell-rich (for making the broth), then it is possible to use a jar of ready made fish soup. But sieve before use as it can often be quite muddy-textured. If you are able to buy canned or bottled mussel juice, that can be good also.

1 x 700g cooked lobster

700g cooked shell-on prawns (these have usually been frozen, but the quality is fine); buy the size that will give you 25–30 prawns per 500g

½ bottle dry white wine

2 kg fresh mussels, cleaned and debearded

1 x 400g can chopped tomatoes

bouquet garni

1 litre shellfish broth (see method), or the bottled soup or mussel stock

2 onions, peeled and finely chopped

3–4 tbsp olive oil

8 very ripe tomatoes, peeled, cored, deseeded and chopped

200g best Arborio rice

4 large fresh scallops, removed from the shell, trimmed and cut into small chunks

2 large cloves garlic, peeled and very
  finely chopped
3 tbsp coarsely chopped flat-leaf parsley

Maldon sea salt and freshly ground
  black pepper

First make the broth. Peel the shells and remove the heads from the lobster and prawns, and put on one side. Cut the lobster flesh into small chunks, put on a plate with the prawn tails and keep cool. Take a large pan and in it boil the white wine for 3–4 minutes. Tip in the mussels and put the lid on. Cook for 30 seconds to 1 minute and drain into a colander – *with another pan underneath* to collect the juices. Shell the mussels when cooler (discard any that have not opened at all) and put onto the same plate as the lobster and prawns. Strain the mussel juices through a fine sieve back into the (cleaned) original pan. Add about 600ml of water, the canned tomatoes and the bouquet garni. Break up the lobster tail with a heavy knife and drop that in too. Simmer, uncovered, for 40 minutes, skimming off any scum that may form in the process. Strain through a colander into yet another pan (you will be wishing you had taken the bottled soup option by now! – but really, this is nicer). Put the prawn tails into a blender, add about 300ml of the cooking liquor and process for 30 seconds. Tip back into the remaining liquor, bring back to a simmer and cook for 5 minutes. Strain through a fine sieve. Measure the liquid. You need about 1 litre.

Have the broth nearby, at the merest simmer. Fry the onions in the olive oil until lightly golden and tip in the tomatoes. Cook for 10–15 minutes until the tomatoes have reduced somewhat and are no longer wet. Add the rice and gently cook with the onions and tomatoes until well coated. Add a ladle of the stock to the rice. Allow to seethe, turn the heat down low and stir gently but purposefully until the liquid has been absorbed into the rice. Only now add some more stock and repeat the process until the stock is used up. Taste some of the rice from time to time as you go. When it is coming close to being ready – still with the *slightest* hardness to the centre of the grain – add a final splash of broth and the scallops. Gently cook them in the rice before adding the cooked shell-fish, garlic and parsley. Heat through thoroughly once more, check for seasoning and serve immediately.

If the rice is cooked before you finish off the stock, don't worry. Conversely, if you think you need more liquid, add a little hot water. A good risotto should be of a lava-like consistency; oozing, and taking a good few seconds before it finally settles on the plate. Never, ever serve Parmesan with a risotto involving fish, it is disgusting and – for me – particularly indigestible.

Asparagus Risotto ⁜ serves 4

One of my all-time favourite risotti. It really is worth making the asparagus-flavoured stock here, as it makes the risotto taste really, really good. The same applies when you decide to make a risotto with peas: keep the pods and boil them up in stock before you start to cook the rice.

1 bundle of asparagus, woody bits chopped off and lower part of stalk trimmed (keep these for flavouring the stock)
700 ml chicken stock
50 g butter
1 medium onion, peeled and finely chopped
4 very thin rashers of rindless streaky bacon, finely sliced into strips

200 g best Arborio rice
150 ml dry white wine
1 tbsp chopped mint
Maldon sea salt and freshly ground black pepper
25 g extra butter
4 tbsp or more freshly grated Parmesan

Put the asparagus trimmings in with the stock and allow to simmer for 30 minutes. Strain through a fine sieve, making sure you press down well on the debris to extract maximum flavour. Keep on a low light at the back of the stove. Chop the main stalks of the asparagus into thick slivers, cut on the diagonal, but leave the tips in their whole shape. Quickly boil these tips in plenty of boiling salted water, for about 2 minutes, until *just* tender. Refresh under cold running water for a few seconds, drain and dry on kitchen paper. Reserve.

In a heavy-based saucepan, melt the butter and fry the onion and bacon until the onions are pale, pale golden and the bacon a bit frizzled. Add the rice and stir around over a meagre flame until well coated with the butter. Pour in the white wine and allow to bubble gently until evaporated. Add the slivers of asparagus stalk and stir in. Now, keeping the pot on a low light, start to add the hot stock, a ladleful at a time, allowing each addition to be fully absorbed before introducing the next, and constantly stirring gently with a wooden spoon. Add the reserved asparagus tips about two-thirds of the way through the cooking process.

Check the texture of the rice as you go along, by eating a bit; it should be cooked through yet firm, but not 'chalky' in the middle, and you may not need all the stock. The resultant texture should be sloppy but not soupy. My ideal description of a perfect risotto is that when it is spooned onto the plate, it should still keep moving for a few seconds, like an exhausted lava flow.

Add the mint and stir in, check for seasoning before adding salt, but grind in plenty of pepper. Take the pot from the heat, stir in the extra butter and cover for 5 minutes. Mix in 1 tbsp or so of the Parmesan and serve onto hot plates, handing extra cheese at table.

Tagliarini con Zucchini   serves 2

Any green vegetable can be cooked with pasta, but the beauty of this one is that as courgettes cook so quickly, they can simply be cooked in the same frying pan as the pasta, once it has been boiled. Tagliarini, a thinner version of tagliatelle, is aesthetically the right one to use here, as it will hold the strips of courgettes better than the more stringlike spaghetti; shapes and dimensions are very important when it comes to cooking with pasta.

200g dried tagliarini
4 medium courgettes, coarsely grated
2–3 tbsp virgin olive oil
Maldon sea salt and freshly ground
   black pepper

2 cloves garlic, peeled and finely
   chopped
freshly grated Parmesan

Cook the pasta in plenty of salted boiling water until *al dente*. Drain thoroughly in a colander and rinse with warm water. Briefly fry the courgettes in 2 tbsp of the oil, with some seasoning and the garlic, in a roomy frying pan until wilted and lightly coloured. Tip in the tagliarini with the remaining oil and turn and toss together until well mixed, and until the pasta has taken on some colour too. Turn onto very hot plates and sprinkle with plenty of freshly grated Parmesan.

Spaghetti with Artichokes, Garlic and Lemon ‡ serves 4

It is the case that most pasta is bought dried in packets. The quality of these can be exceptionally good, with Cipriani and De Cecco brands being particularly fine. Also, certain dishes like the wonderfully simple Sicilian *spaghetti al aglio, olio e peperoncino* (spaghetti with garlic, olive oil and dried chillies) would not work correctly with floppy and tender home-made pasta; it needs the sprightliness and almost chewiness of dried pasta to make the dish a success. The same applies here.

*8 large globe artichoke hearts, trimmed
 of all leaves and choke, pared down
 to the hearts and thinly sliced
4 tbsp olive oil
Maldon sea salt and freshly ground
 black pepper
4 cloves garlic, peeled and thinly sliced*

*grated rind and juice of 1 lemon
250g dried spaghetti
2–3 tbsp extra-virgin olive oil
freshly ground black pepper
a little chopped mint
freshly grated Parmesan*

Have a large pan of salted water at a simmer. Take a large frying pan, and in it fry the artichokes in the 4 tbsp olive oil until golden. Season, add the garlic and continue cooking for a minute or two. Squeeze in the lemon juice and keep warm on one side (or in a low oven with the door ajar). Turn up the heat under the simmering water until boiling fast. Put in the pasta, cook until *al dente* (just a little bit firm to the tooth) and drain well.

Tip into a large preheated bowl, add the 2–3 tbsp extra-virgin olive oil and plenty of freshly ground black pepper. Toss well and divide between 4 hot plates. Top each serving with the artichokes, sprinkle over the mint and grated lemon rind and serve immediately. Hand the Parmesan separately.

Linguine with Squid and Chillies ‡ serves 2

Soon after my friend Alastair Little opened his second restaurant in Lancaster Road, in Notting Hill, west London (his first and eponymous Alastair Little in Soho, already established and much renowned), I ventured along there with a friend one night and enjoyed this dish of pasta with squid. It was so very, very good, that I was moved to order it up a second time. His chef at that moment, the talented Toby Gush, was the man who actually cooked it, but Al's stamp was all over it. The following recipe is my interpretation; I just hope it is as good for you as it was for me.

Appropriately – and not surprisingly – the west London branch is called Alastair Little Lancaster Road.

200g spaghetti (use Di Cecco or
    Cipriani brands, not home-made;
    it is too soft and will break up)
350g squid, uncleaned weight (ask
    your fishmonger to clean and gut
    the squid)

3 tbsp olive oil
3 cloves garlic, peeled and sliced
½ tsp (or more) dried chilli flakes
Maldon sea salt
juice of ½ a lemon
1 tbsp chopped flat-leaf parsley

In a large pan of salted boiling water, cook the spaghetti for 6–7 minutes, until just cooked but firm. Drain in a colander and refresh well under cold running water. Slice the squid bodies in half lengthways, and then into thin strips. If the tentacles are big, cut them in half.

Put a large non-stick frying pan on to heat and add 1 tbsp of the olive oil. Heat until smoking, then throw in the squid. Stir-fry briskly for about 2 minutes, and tip onto a plate. Lower the heat, add the remaining oil and heat gently this time. Fry the garlic until pale golden and then add the chillies and spaghetti.

Reintroduce the squid, turn up the heat, and stir-fry vigorously until the spaghetti takes on a little colour and becomes deliciously crisp in parts. Season well, squeeze over the lemon juice and throw in the parsley. Serve at once.

Green Lasagne with Mushrooms and Bacon ‡

serves 9 (an odd number, but the dish divides well into that amount)

Franco Taruschio of The Walnut Tree, near Abergavenny, in Wales (of whose recipe for his extraordinary *Vincis Grassi* I am unashamedly about to doctor), climbs up into the hills near his restaurant as often as is possible, to stock up his cavernous freezer with ceps – or *porcini*, as he would say.

One day, he invited me along too. He picked 9 kilos, I picked 1½. He laughed and most generously gave me some of his to take home. He later (also very generously) allowed me to become really quite drunk on some home-made grappa a friend had given him in Italy. It was flavoured with caraway. Caraway? I was the one carried away . . .

As I previously mentioned, this first recipe is an adaptation of Franco's extraordinary *Vincis Grassi Maceratese*, which involves layers of lasagne, rich béchamel, *porcini*, prosciutto and truffles. It is beyond belief good. My lowlier version involves some similar ingredients (apart from the truffles), but has a generous quality about it. Just like Franco, really.

For the béchamel:
1 litre milk
4 cloves
1 large onion, peeled and chopped
2 bay leaves
Maldon sea salt

100g butter
100g plain flour
275ml single cream
freshly grated nutmeg
freshly ground black pepper

For the lasagne:

*200g dried green lasagne – about
    9 sheets*
700g large flat black mushrooms
a little olive oil
juice of 1 lemon
2 cloves garlic
*225g bacon (I use thinly sliced
    Italian pancetta, which you can*
*buy from some supermarkets now.
    Failing that, use tasty streaky
    bacon)*
2 tbsp chopped oregano
4 tbsp freshly grated Parmesan
75g butter
1 bunch sage, leaves only

It is almost essential to use one of those heat-diffuser pads for cooking the béchamel sauce, as it scorches easily. Also, use a heavy-bottomed saucepan.

Heat together the milk, cloves, onion, bay leaves and a little salt. Simmer for a few minutes, cover and allow the flavours to mingle for about 30 minutes. In another pan, melt the butter and stir in the flour. Make a roux and gently cook the butter and flour together for a minute or two, but on no account allow it to colour; it must stay pale. But it *is* important that the flour cooks. Strain the milk into the roux and vigorously whisk together until smooth (this always gets rid of any lumps). On the lowest possible heat (preferably with a heat-diffuser pad), set the sauce to cook. You may think that the sauce is very thick to begin with. However, as it cooks, the consistency will become silky and unctuous and, remember, there is some cream to add at the end. Do not cover the sauce, stir, from time to time, with a wooden spoon and cook for about 1 hour. Add the cream, nutmeg and pepper, mix in thoroughly, check for salt and cook for a further 5 minutes. Strain again into a clean pan and put a lid on (this helps to prevent a skin forming). Set aside and keep warm.

Preheat the oven to 400°F/205°C/gas mark 6.

Cook the sheets of lasagne in well-salted boiling water until just firm. Drain, rinse briefly under cold running water and lay out onto a clean tea towel. Put the mushrooms onto a roasting tray that will take them quite tightly packed. Drizzle each mushroom with some olive oil and squeeze over the lemon juice. Slice the garlic into bits, tuck under the mushrooms and season. Bake in the oven for 30–40 minutes until well cooked, and when cool slice in half *horizontally*. Grill the *pancetta* or bacon carefully until crisp.

To assemble, take a rectangular metal tin or shallow plastic box and smear the base with some of the béchamel. Put in a layer of lasagne and then another thin coating of béchamel. Sprinkle with 1 tbsp of the oregano. Cover with a layer of half the mushrooms, add a little more béchamel and then half the bacon. Now cover with another layer of lasagne. Repeat this process. It is important that the top layer is lasagne, and well covered with a final layer of béchamel. Cover the surface with clingfilm and put into the fridge for at least 6 hours or overnight, to set.

Preheat the oven to 400°F/205°C/gas mark 6.

With a sharp knife, cut the lasagne into 9 equal portions. Carefully lift out with a fish slice and lay onto a flat baking tray with space in between the portions (use two trays if one is too small). Evenly sprinkle the surface of each with the Parmesan. Bake in the oven for 30 minutes until the surfaces are bubbling and golden. Meanwhile melt the butter until foaming and fry the sage leaves until crisp. Season with a little salt. Using a fish slice, transfer the lasagne to individual hot plates and spoon a little of the sage leaves and butter over each serving. Hand more Parmesan separately if desired.

The dish is a rich one and only needs an accompanying crisp green salad, if that. I would find it too much for a first course, but if that might be what you wish to do, then this recipe would obviously feed more.

Pastry

Tomato and Saffron Quiche ‡ serves 6

The quiche from Lorraine remains my best beloved, with its particular savour remaining unmatched. However, the following rich pale orange-tinged custard which sets to a tremble in thin and crisp pastry comes a close second.

I was inspired to put these two simple flavours together after having learnt to make a sumptuous shellfish quiche that we used to make at the Normandie Restaurant, Birtle, near Bury, in Lancashire, where I learnt to cook in the early 1970s. The tomato, garlic and saffron enhanced the flavours of the shellfish, as much as salt and vinegar do to a wrapping of fish and chips.

A more perfect supper for a vegetarian I cannot imagine.

For the pastry:
50g butter, cut into cubes
100g plain flour
a pinch of salt
1–2 tbsp iced water
a little beaten egg

For the filling:
400ml double cream

1 tsp saffron threads, steeped in 1 tbsp
  hot water for 5 minutes
2 eggs
4 egg yolks
12 leaves basil, coarsely chopped
a little Maldon sea salt and freshly
  ground black pepper
2 x 400g tins chopped tomatoes
2 cloves garlic, peeled and finely
  chopped

In a food processor, electric mixer or manually, blend together the butter, flour and salt until it resembles fine breadcrumbs. Now tip into a large, roomy bowl and gently mix in the water and egg yolk with cool hands or a knife, until well amalgamated. Put into a plastic bag and chill in the fridge for at least 1 hour before rolling.

Put the tomatoes, garlic and seasoning in a stainless-steel pan and allow to simmer for a good 30 minutes or so, at least until the mixture is well reduced and jammy, as it needs to be spread onto the pastry base, and must not be sloppy.

Preheat the oven to 350°F/180°C/gas mark 4.

Roll out the pastry as thinly as possible, line a 20 cm × 4 cm tart tin and bake blind. This is achieved by lining the uncooked pastry case with a sheet of tin foil and filling with some dried haricot beans, for instance. It is then cooked for about 15–20 minutes, removed from the oven, and the foil and beans transferred to a bowl or tin (for future use). Brush the inside of the case with the beaten egg, which will form a seal and prevent any leaks. Return to the oven for a further 10 minutes or so, until it is golden, crisp and well cooked through, particularly the base.

Put 3–4 tbsp of the cream in a small pan together with the saffron. Warm through and leave to infuse for 5 minutes. Beat together the eggs and yolks and pour in the remaining cream and the saffron cream. *Note:* Do not use a whisk now, as all the saffron threads will curl themselves around it. So stir well with a wooden spoon and add seasoning. Stir in the basil, and season.

Turn the oven down to 325°F/160°C/gas mark 3.

To assemble the tart, spread the tomato over the tart base and then pour in the saffron custard. Fill the case as full as you dare – there is nothing sadder than a half-filled quiche – and if you find it easier, then fill half the case first and the rest once it is in the oven. Use a deep spoon or ladle for this last bit. Bake for 30–40 minutes until set and pale golden brown on the surface. Allow to cool for at least 10 minutes before eating, as hot quiche tastes of very little.

Lancashire Meat Pie ‡ serves 6

I always used to hanker after meat pies that I'd see in northern baker's shops when I was a kid. They were also to be seen on stalls at Bury market too, between the black pudding stall and the one that only sold Lancashire cheese and eggs. That Lancashire cheese, by the way, remains the finest I have ever tasted. Great lumps of it, stacked in massive wedges and wheels, its odour wafting on the air all sour-smelling and deeply lactic. The woman who sold it, strong of voice and with a jolly pink face, was forever demanding which particular Lancashire it was you wanted. It went something like this: 'Well, there's crumbly mild, dear, or crumbly tasty.

Then there's creamy tasty or creamy mild; or crumbly creamy, extra tasty and then there's eggs too . . . Here, there's a bit of cheese for you, my duck.'

Then there was the frightening-looking red-haired woman on a vegetable stall, whom my mother referred to as Mad Annie. She could shout the peel off a King Edward at fifty paces. I remember asking one day, a little too loudly – 'Is that Mad Annie, Mum? Is it? *Is it?*' The sharp look (it was a sharpish face) I was given was enough to make me cross my legs and talk aimlessly to our dog. It irritated Mother no end to have to get her greens elsewhere after that little episode. Oh, the shame!

But, you see, I never did get to eat those meat pies, because Mum always made her own, which were really, really great. But I always had – and still have – a longing for shop-bought, home-made pies: Cornish pasties fresh from the oven at the Rock Bakery, just across the estuary from Padstow in Cornwall, pork pies in Melton Mowbray, good home-made sausage rolls, and Bakewell puddings from Bakewell in Derbyshire. I also have a worrying penchant for Fray Bentos Steak and Kidney Pies too . . .

I have used my imagination here as to what I think these should have tasted like. The inclusion of a little potato serves to bulk out the meat somewhat and also tastes really good.

You will need a loose-bottomed pastry tin measuring 20 cm × 4 cm, lightly buttered, and a flat oven tray. This is put in the oven to heat up, so that the base of the pie will cook through evenly.

For the pastry:
200g dripping or lard, very cold from the fridge and cut into small pieces
350g plain flour
Maldon sea salt
6 tbsp ice-cold water

For the filling:
600g stewing steak (make sure it has bits of fat and sinew in it), cut into small dice
350g chopped onion
300g diced peeled potato
Maldon sea salt and plenty of freshly ground white pepper
1 level tbsp plain flour
200ml water
a little beaten egg and milk

To make the pastry, rub together the fat, flour and salt until it resembles coarse breadcrumbs. Quickly mix in the water and work together to a coherent mass. Knead lightly and put into a plastic bag. Leave to rest in the fridge until the filling has been prepared.

Preheat the oven to 400°F/205°C/gas mark 6, and put the baking tray onto the middle shelf.

Put all the ingredients (except the water and egg wash) for the filling into a roomy bowl and mix together well with your hands.

Divide the pastry into two-thirds and one-third size pieces. Roll the larger into a circle about 0.5 cm thick – it does not want to be too thin. Line the tin, leaving the over-hang intact. Roll out the rest of the pastry for the lid and set aside. Pile the filling in right to the top (it will all go in, don't worry) and carefully pour in the water, which should just reach the surface. Brush the edge of the overhanging pastry with water and put on the lid. Press the edges together at the rim of the tin and then slice off the excess pastry with a knife all in one go.

Brush the surface with the egg wash, and then decorate and further press the edges together with the tines of a fork. Make two generous incisions in the centre of the pie and place in the oven. Cook for 25 minutes, and then turn the temperature down to 325°F/160°C/gas mark 3. Bake for a further 1½ hours, checking from time to time that the pastry is not browning too much. If it is, then turn the oven down a little more. What makes this sort of pie so special is a long, slow cooking, with all the elements cooking as one. To be truly authentic, eat with a splash of malt vinegar and some piccalilli or ketchup.

Flamiche ⚜ serves 4, generously

The small town of Roye, about an hour's drive north of Paris, was a brief map-folding off the autoroute, and locals were clearly all enjoying lunch as we pulled into the deserted square. The restaurant, La Flamiche – for that was the name of the singly stellated establishment, favoured by the little red book, and to which our rumbling tummies had alerted my friend

Lindsey Bareham and me – appeared plain and serious on its corner of the square. We liked that.

One of the specialities listed in the good book was, naturally, *La Flamiche aux Poireaux*: a buttery leek pie – a famed speciality of Alsatian cookery. Imagine our disappointment on discovering that said flamiche was unavailable due to seasonal unavailability of leeks . . . Fifty kilometres of salivation instantaneously quashed in the shaking of a napkin. *Tant pis*, as they say, but hats off to Alsatian proprietors M. et Mme Klopp for respecting the seasons. Pish!

At supermarkets you can now buy ready rolled circles of fresh puff pastry. The ones I have found have been of good quality and weigh in at 250g a piece. You will need two of these, which is just perfect for this recipe. Note: You will also need *two* flat baking trays (with no edges).

75g butter
1 kg leeks, trimmed of most of the green, trimmed, sliced and well washed
Maldon sea salt, freshly ground black pepper and freshly grated nutmeg

5–6 tbsp double cream
500g puff pastry
1 egg yolk, beaten

Melt the butter in a wide frying pan and cook the leeks gently, for about 20 minutes until really soft. Season, turn up the heat, and add the cream. Allow to bubble vigorously for a minute or two until the mixture is creamy, but not too wet. Tip onto a plate and allow to cool.

Preheat the oven to 425°F/220°C/gas mark 7.

Place one of the baking trays into the oven to get hot. Lightly smear the other one with butter and on it lay one of the circles of puff pastry. Take the cooled leeks and spread them carefully into a piled, though flattish, circle over the pastry, leaving an edge of 2.5cm uncovered; paint this with egg yolk. Form a lid with the other circle of pastry and allow the edge of this to flop down onto the bottom layer. Press together lightly all the way around. Now brush the whole surface with more egg wash and press the edges together firmly with the tines of a fork. Also, make a few

Left: Flamiche

small cuts in the centre of the *flamiche*, so as to allow steam to escape. Decorate with the point of a knife if you are in an artistic mood.

Slide the *flamiche* in to the oven, onto the preheated tray. Bake for around 25 minutes or until golden brown and well crisped. Allow to cool for 5 minutes before serving. Cut into wedges and eat with salad or just on its own.

Cheese and Ham Pie ‡ serves 4

The name for this should really read as *Pithiviers au Jambon et Fromage*, as the first time I came across it was at the Boucherie Lamartine, in Ebury Street, London SW1, several years ago. It has since been renamed and is now called the House of Albert Roux. The shop is owned by the eponymous and legendary man himself, and orchestrated by resident chef and *charcutier* Michael Aldridge, who kindly furnished me with this super recipe.

As I mentioned in the recipe for *Flamiche* (page 167) it is now possible to buy ready-rolled fresh puff pastry circles from supermarkets. As in the recipe for Lancashire Meat Pie (page 165), it is best to place a flat baking sheet in the oven to preheat before putting in the pie.

For the béchamel sauce:
400ml milk
2 cloves
1 onion, peeled and chopped
1 bay leaf
Maldon sea salt
75g butter
50g plain flour
150ml single cream
freshly grated nutmeg
freshly ground black pepper

150g Gruyère or Emmental cheese,
    coarsely grated

For the pie:
500g puff pastry (2 thinly rolled
    circles, weighing 250g each)
500g thinly sliced cooked ham, the
    finest you can find
1 egg yolk, beaten with a pinch of
    salt and 1 tsp water, for glazing
    the pie

First make the béchamel sauce. Heat together the milk, cloves, onion, bay leaf and a little salt. Simmer for a few minutes, cover and allow the flavours to mingle for about 15 minutes. In another pan, melt the butter and stir in the flour. Make a roux and gently cook the butter and flour together for a minute or two, but do not allow to colour. Strain the milk into the roux and vigorously whisk together until smooth. Set the sauce to cook very gently (preferably on a diffuser pad) for about 15 minutes, stirring occasionally. You may think that the sauce is very thick to begin with. However, as it cooks, the consistency will become silky and unctuous and, remember, there is still some cream to add.

Add the cream, nutmeg and pepper, mix in thoroughly, check for salt and cook for a further minute or two. Strain into a bowl, cover the surface with clingfilm and put in the fridge to cool completely. Once cold, stir in the cheese. It is important that the sauce is fully cold, as the cheese should not melt until it is inside the pie whilst it bakes.

Lightly grease a second flat baking sheet and lay upon it one of the circles of puff pastry. Take the other sheet of pastry and roll it out a little thinner, so that it is about 2.5 cm wider than the other. Leave to rest in the fridge. Now place a slice of ham upon the pastry on the tray, so that it comes to within 1.5 cm of the edge. Spread with a very thin layer of the béchamel/cheese mixture and then add another slice of ham. Keep doing this until both ham and sauce are all used up, ending with a slice of ham. Brush the exposed edge of pastry with a little of the egg wash and lay over the larger circle of pastry. Lightly press the edges together with your fingers.

Brush the whole surface of the pie with egg wash and then decorate the edge with the tines of a fork, or form a scalloped edge, which is particularly traditional for a *pithiviers*. Also, using the side of the blade of a small pointed knife, make spiral lines, starting at the centre and sweeping down to the edge, ending up measuring about 2cm apart. Be careful, however, not to cut into the pastry. Preheat the oven to 400°F/205°C/gas mark 6. Leave to rest for 30 minutes. Bake for 30–40 minutes until golden and puffed up. Cut into wedges and eat warm, with a pint of beer.

Chocolate *Pithiviers* ✣ serves 6

The following dessert I first ate at Michel Guérard's restaurant, at Eugénie-les-Bains in south-west France, some years ago now. It is something that I played around with for years before getting it right. M. Guérard, being the genius that he is, was conveniently lost for words when it came to giving me the exact recipe. So naturally, I was forced to try to improve the dish. I think – and hope – it came out OK in the end. Thankfully, it seems that guests at Bibendum have been enjoying it over the past eleven years, where it has been on the dessert menu since day one.

For the *crème pâtissière*:
250ml milk
1 vanilla pod, split lengthways
3 egg yolks
75g caster sugar
25g plain flour

For the chocolate mixture:
100g unsalted butter, softened
100g caster sugar
2 small eggs

100g ground almonds
50g cocoa powder
½ tbsp dark rum
100g plain bitter chocolate, chopped
    into tiny pieces or good quality
    chocolate chips
1 x 350g pkt puff pastry (fresh or
    frozen from the supermarket,
    or home-made)
beaten egg, to glaze
icing sugar, for dusting

First make the *crème pâtissière*. Put the milk in a saucepan with the vanilla pod and heat gently to boiling point. Whisk together the egg yolks, sugar and flour. Pour the hot milk onto the egg mixture and beat together lightly. Return the mixture to the saucepan and cook gently until thickened. Pour through a sieve, remove the vanilla pod (reserve for another time), then chill.

For the chocolate mixture, cream the butter and sugar together until light and fluffy. Add the eggs and beat again. Now pour in the almonds and cocoa powder. Beat again. Add the rum, together with the *crème pâtissière*, and finally fold in the chocolate. Chill.

Preheat the oven to 400°F/205°C/gas mark 6. Roll out the pastry very thinly and cut into 12 pieces, half 10 cm x 10 cm and half 15 cm x 15 cm.

Place the 6 smaller squares on a floured surface. Using a large ice-cream scoop (for instance) place a scoop of the chocolate mixture in the centre of each. Brush the edges with half of the beaten egg, put the larger squares of pastry on top and press down and around firmly, making sure there are no air bubbles trapped inside.

Using a 10 cm circumference pastry cutter, cut the filled pastry squares into neat rounds. Discard the trimmings, or use in another dish. Press and seal together the edges with a fork to form a decorative pattern. Brush the *pithiviers* with the remaining beaten egg and dust lightly with icing sugar.

Place on a greased baking sheet and cook in the oven for 15–20 minutes or until the pastry is puffed and golden, shiny and crisp. Remove, dust lightly with more icing sugar and serve hot, with thick cream.

Pastry

Hot Strawberry Pie ⁘ serves 6

This is possibly my most fondly remembered recipe of my mother's. She would always have one ready waiting, warm and weeping pink juice, on the back of the Aga for my first night home from boarding school at the beginning of the summer holidays. In the winter hols, it would be a meat and 'tatie pie.

If you are able to buy slightly over-ripe strawberries for this, then do. They can often be at a bargain price and work just as well as prime specimens.

You will also need a loose-bottomed cake tin measuring 21 cm × 4 cm.

For the pastry:
250g chilled butter, cut into small pieces
500g self-raising flour
a pinch of salt
50ml ice-cold water
1 egg yolk

For the pie:
a little butter
1kg strawberries, hulled and cut in half lengthways
butter
75g caster sugar
1 beaten egg mixed with 1 tbsp of milk

173

In a food processor, electric mixer or manually, blend together the butter, flour and salt until it resembles fine breadcrumbs. Now tip into a large, roomy bowl and gently mix in the water and egg yolk with cool hands or a knife, until amalgamated. (*Note:* I do finally think that this is the best way to bind pastry together. It doesn't get beaten to oblivion by machine and consequently results in light and crisp pastry. The use of self-raising flour also adds lightness.) Put into a plastic bag and chill in the fridge for at least 1 hour before rolling.

Preheat the oven to 400°F/205°C/gas mark 6.

Lightly grease the cake tin with the butter. Roll out two-thirds of the pastry into a circle; don't make it too thin. Carefully line the tin with this, allowing a slight excess to flop over the rim. Tip in the strawberries, sprinkle over 60 g of the sugar and shake the tin slightly so that the sugar disperses. Lightly press down with your hands. Now brush a little of the beaten egg and milk around the edge of the pastry that lies just above the rim of the cake tin. Roll out the remaining one-third of pastry, but slightly thinner than the base. Carefully lift onto the pie and, with your fingers, lightly press the two pastry edges together. Then, with a sharp knife, cut through the joined edges almost flush up to the rim. Now knock the edges together, again with your fingers, to form a crinkled edge all the way around (you may use the scraps to make some artful decorations on the lid if you feel moved so to do). Brush the whole surface with more of the beaten egg and milk and evenly sprinkle with the remaining caster sugar. Make a couple of incisions in the centre of the pastry lid to allow steam to escape.

Put into the oven on the middle shelf with an empty roasting tin underneath. The reason for the tin is to catch any dribbles that almost certainly will ooze out of the pie as it cooks, so make sure that the roasting tin is larger than the pie! These juices may burn a little, so watch out. Cook for about 15 minutes at this temperature and then turn down to 325°F/160°C/gas mark 3 for a further 30–40 minutes. Take from the oven when the pastry is a rich golden colour and put on a large round plate. Leave in the tin until lukewarm, before removing. Cut into wedges and serve with clotted or whipped cream.

Gooseberry Pie ‡ serves 6

Another of Mum's good pies. The gooseberries came from our garden, all hairy and tart, and it was usually me who was sent to pick them. We would then top and tail them together, sitting in green deckchairs on the lawn, with a colander to throw them into. I fondly remember how the first few went *ping-ping* as they hit the empty vessel.

Use the same pastry for this as for the Strawberry Pie (page 173) and also the same sort of tin. The procedure for assembly is also identical.

1 batch of pastry (as for the Strawberry Pie)
1 kg gooseberries, topped and tailed and left whole
225g caster sugar
50g softened butter
1 beaten egg mixed with 1 tbsp milk

Once the cake tin is lined with pastry, add a single layer of the gooseberries, strew with some of the sugar and add a few flecks of butter. Continue like this until the fruit, sugar and butter are used up. Top with the pastry, and cook, as for the Strawberry Pie. Serve lukewarm and with cream. This particular pie should ideally be accompanied by some sweet Alsatian wine, such as a late harvest Gewürztraminer or Muscat. The affinity is notable.

Eccles Cakes ‡ makes about 15 cakes

An English pastry that used to be truly wonderful. Sadly this has now become just another rather dry, sweet pastry, mostly commercially made, with nowhere near enough of the black wet mass of currants that should out-do the pastry wrapping to about the ratio of 10–1; at least that is what I have found over their declining years. The recipe that follows will hopefully remind you of what they used to be like.

It is fine to use frozen puff pastry here, particularly as it is rolled quite thinly. However, home-made – if you are good at making it – would make superlative Eccles cakes, to be sure.

For the fruit filling:
75g butter
2 tbsp brandy
75g soft brown sugar
225g currants
4 globes preserved stem ginger, finely
    chopped
3 tbsp ginger syrup (from the jar)
1 tsp mixed spice

½ tsp powdered ginger
grated rind and juice of 1 lemon
grated rind of 1 orange

To assemble:
1 × 350g puff pastry
a little beaten egg
a little milk
flour and caster sugar, for dusting

Melt the butter and add the brandy to it. Whilst still on the heat, add the sugar and dissolve. With the mixture still warm, add all the other filling ingredients and stir well. Leave to soak and cool, for at least 1 hour, before using.

Preheat the oven to 400°F/205°C/gas mark 6.

Roll the pastry out thinly, to about 3mm. Cut into circles about 10cm in diameter and place 1 dsp of the mixture in the centre of each. Brush the rim of the pastry circle with a little egg wash, lift up two edges to the centre and press together. Then take the remaining edges and lift over on top. Press lightly together. Dust with flour and turn over. Roll out lightly to flatten a little and then form into as neat a circle as you can; the result should resemble a little pie. Cut two or three traditional little slashes in the top, brush with a little milk and lightly dust with caster sugar. Continue making the Eccles cakes until both the pastry and filling are used up.

Lay the cakes on a greased baking tray and bake on the middle shelf of the oven for 15–20 minutes, or until puffed a little, glossy and golden brown. Cool on a cake rack and eat whilst still lukewarm.

Left: Eccles Cakes

Simple Almond Tart   serves 4–5

This is the easiest of tarts to make and is best eaten warm, with thick cream. It has a similarity, in the ingredients, with a traditional Bakewell Pudding, but is not as rich. I once used marmalade in the base of the tart, instead of the more traditional apricot jam, which was a huge success, but you could use any sort of jam that happens to be around.

For the pastry:
50g butter, cut into cubes
100g plain flour
a pinch of salt
1–2 tbsp iced water
1 egg yolk

For the filling:
100g softened butter
100g caster sugar
2 large eggs
100g ground almonds
grated rind of 1 lemon

a little beaten egg
2 tbsp jam

First make the pastry. In a food processor, electric mixer or manually, blend together the butter, flour and salt until it resembles fine bread-crumbs. Now tip into a large, roomy bowl and gently mix in the water and egg yolk with cool hands or a knife, until well amalgamated. Put into a plastic bag and chill in the fridge for at least 1 hour before rolling out.

Preheat the oven to 350°F/180°C/gas mark 4.

Roll out the pastry as thinly as possible, line a loose-bottomed 20 cm × 4 cm tart tin and bake blind. This is achieved by lining the uncooked pastry case with a sheet of tin foil and filling with some dried haricot beans, for instance. It is then cooked for about 15–20 minutes, removed from the oven, and the foil and beans transferred to a bowl or tin (for future use). Brush the inside of the case with the beaten egg, which will form a seal and prevent any leaks. Return to the oven for a further 10 minutes or so, until it is golden, crisp and well cooked through, particularly the base. Warm the jam slightly and spoon over the base of the tart. Leave to cool in the tin.

For the filling, beat together the butter and sugar, preferably in an electric mixer, until light and fluffy. Add 1 egg and continue beating until entirely incorporated, then add the other and beat again. Add the almonds and lemon rind and carefully, but thoroughly, fold them in.

Spoon into the tart case and smooth the top. Place in the oven (at the same temperature) on the middle shelf and bake for 40 minutes or so, until the surface is golden brown, puffed up and springy to the touch. Switch off the oven and leave to cool there with the door ajar, for 15 minutes. Dust with caster sugar before serving.

Puddings

Jamaican Ginger Cake Pudding   ☧   serves 4

I have always had a penchant for packaged cakes and pastries. Mr Kipling's Treacle Tart is good, though not as good as it was when there were no silly strips of lattice pastry over the surface, as there are now. What is the point? – it hinders the filling in the most annoying way.

I can also eat a whole packet of the American Oreo cookies in seconds flat, but they must be accompanied by a large glass of ice-cold milk for best effect. Battenburgs, iced almond slices (reeking of almond essence), Viennese whirls and slices of moist Malt Loaf spread with salty butter all take my fancy too. And McVitie's Jamaican Ginger Cake is possibly the finest of all. I really don't think I could ever make one as good – but then I have never been that much of an expert when it comes to baking. There is also another one available now, which is very similar to the ginger cake: the McVitie's Golden Syrup Cake!

Now this is something else, I thought, until I discovered – tucked alongside their Mummies and Daddies on the shelf – little boy-and-girl-size Golden Syrup cakes and Jamaican Ginger Cakes. But oh no, it didn't stop there. These diminutive, individually wrapped cakes have a line of Golden Syrup running through the middle of one, and a similar channel of gingery goo forced into the other. An idea started to form in my greedy head and I promptly bought two of each.

I put the steamer together that evening (one of those dirt-cheap Chinese jobbies, two layers and made of cheap aluminium; every home should have one), hurriedly ripped open one of each cake, wrapped them in foil and steamed them for 30 minutes. They smelt absolutely marvellous when I unwrapped them. Into a dish they went, drowned in very cold pouring cream and . . . mmmmm . . . yum.

Well, a little work was still necessary to actually make a proper pudding. So I reverted to the grown-up Jamaican Ginger Cake, thought of bread and butter pudding, and the following recipe is the result. It is a lovely instant pudding if you always have one of those cakes to hand (they keep for ages). But then each and every corner shop always seems to have them in stock.

For the pudding:
50g softened butter
1 McVitie's Jamaican Ginger Cake,
    cut into 2cm thick slices
5 globes stem ginger, cut into chunks
2 tbsp dark rum
175ml milk
1 small egg
2 small egg yolks
2 tbsp stem ginger syrup from the jar
150ml double cream
a pinch of salt

1 tsp pure vanilla extract
a little sifted icing sugar

For the *crème Chantilly*:
150ml whipping cream, very well
    chilled
150ml double cream, very well
    chilled
40g sifted icing sugar
vanilla seeds scraped from a split ½ of
    a fresh vanilla pod

Lightly grease a suitable baking dish with a little of the butter, and use the rest to spread over the slices of Ginger Cake. Lay into the dish, slightly overlapping, and push the chunks of ginger into the cake with the point of a small knife. Spoon over the rum. Scald the milk. Beat together the egg and egg yolks with the ginger syrup and add the milk, cream, salt and vanilla extract. Pour over the cake and leave to soak for about 30 minutes. Preheat the oven to 350°F/180°C/gas mark 4.

Bake on the middle shelf of the oven for 30–40 minutes until the custard mixture has just set and has taken on a pale golden sheen around the edges. Remove from the oven and leave to stand for about 15 minutes, as the pudding is best eaten warm.

Meanwhile, make the *crème Chantilly*. It is important that all is cold for this most lovely of whipped creams; it allows for the least chance of the cream separating whilst being beaten. Put everything in a (preferably metal) bowl that has been in the freezer for 30 minutes and hand-whisk the cream using fluid motions until loosely thick, but on no account very thick. This does not take as long as you would think it might. And it is a special further pleasure to see the difference between hand-whisked, as opposed to electrically aided beaten cream.

Just prior to serving, dust the pudding with the sifted icing sugar.

Steamed Ginger Pudding ‡ serves 6

One of my more embarrassing moments – which occurred during my first few weeks of writing my *Independent* column – was when I gave a recipe for this steamed ginger pudding. The amounts of bicarb and baking powder that I suggested were given as tablespoons rather than teaspoons! You can imagine the result: rather salty and really quite well risen . . .

100g plain flour
2 tsp ground ginger
1 tsp mixed spice
1 tsp baking powder
1 tsp bicarbonate of soda
100g suet
100g fresh breadcrumbs

1 × 165g jar preserved stem ginger
    and its syrup
200ml milk
50g Golden Syrup
75g treacle or molasses
a pinch of salt
butter

Sift the flour into a mixing bowl with the spices and raising agents. Add the suet and breadcrumbs and mix well. Coarsely chop the stem ginger and its syrup in the bowl of a food processor. Warm the milk with half the stem ginger and syrup, the Golden Syrup, the treacle or molasses and a pinch of salt. Beat into the dry ingredients until sloppy and just dropping off the spoon. Add the salt and mix well. Generously grease a 1 litre pudding basin with butter and put the remaining stem ginger and syrup in the bottom. Pour in the pudding mixture, cover with buttered foil, and steam for 2 hours. Turn out onto a dish and serve with very cold thick cream or custard.

Apple Hat ‡ serves 6

The first time I ever ate an Apple Hat was at Rules restaurant in Covent Garden. It was beautifully turned out, a little individual steaming damp dome sitting in a moat of yellow custard. With this family recipe, the hat is at least a size 6- rather than that of an infant's pate. I am indebted here

to Sara Paston-Williams' marvellous *Book of Traditional Puddings*, published by the National Trust some years ago but now sadly out of print.

225g self-raising flour	*3 cloves*
a pinch of salt	*a generous pinch of cinnamon*
125g shredded suet	*a generous pinch of ground ginger*
6–8 tbsp cold water	*grated rind and juice of ½ a lemon*
700g cooking apples (Bramleys)	*or orange*
50g raisins or sultanas	*50g unsalted butter*
75g soft brown sugar	*1 tbsp clotted cream*

Generously butter a 1 litre pudding basin. Sift the flour with the salt into a mixing bowl. Stir in the suet and mix with sufficient cold water to make a soft, light dough. Knead lightly and roll out onto a floured board to a thickness of about 0.5cm. Use two-thirds of the pastry to line the prepared basin.

Peel, core and slice the apples and fill the lined basin with layers of apples, raisins or sultanas, sugar and spices. Add the lemon or orange rind and juice and the butter, cut into small pieces. Cover the basin with the reserved pastry, dampening the edges and pressing together firmly. Cover with a piece of well-buttered, pleated greaseproof paper followed by a piece of similarly buttered foil with a further pleat, but placed at right-angles to the greaseproof, so as to allow the pudding to rise. Tie around securely with string. Steam for 2–2½ hours.

Turn out onto a warmed serving plate and remove a piece of the pastry from the (now) top of the pudding. Pop in the clotted cream, which will melt into the pudding. Serve hot with more cream and brown sugar or with custard.

Left: **Apple Hat**

Pear Clafoutis   ‡   serves 4

The original recipe for this involved the use of honey as a sweetener. As I have never really liked honey, I thought it best to delete it. However, if you like it, then by all means replace the sugar with its weight in honey. And, by the way, I am also not the biggest fan of *clafoutis* that are cooked in a pastry case. I do not know where this curious aberration originated, but I am here to say that it needs a good stamping on. *Clafoutis*, in essence, is nothing more than a sweetened batter pudding, although this recipe is a little more sophisticated than that rather mundane description.

25g butter	*a tiny pinch of salt*
500g ripe pears, peeled, cored and cut into small pieces	*1 tsp potato flour (fécule de pommes de terre)*
100g caster sugar	*250ml whipping cream*
1 whole egg, separated	*1 tbsp flaked almonds (optional)*
2 egg yolks	*a little sifted icing sugar*
1 tsp pure almond essence	

Melt half the butter in a non-stick pan and add the pears. Sprinkle with 25g of the sugar and gently stew the pears for a few minutes until sticky and pale golden. Use the remaining butter to grease a fairly deep oval oven dish, scrape the pears into it, and put on one side.

Preheat the oven to 350°F/180°C/gas mark 4.

Beat together the egg yolks, 50g of the sugar, the almond essence, salt and the potato flour. Stir in the cream and incorporate thoroughly. Briefly whisk the egg white with the remaining 25g sugar until glossy, and fold into the custard mixture. Pour over the pears and place the dish into a roasting tin. Add water to the roasting tin until it comes at least three-quarters of the way up the side of the dish. Sprinkle the surface of the *clafoutis* with the almonds if using, and sift a little icing sugar on top. Carefully slide into the oven and bake for 20–25 minutes until slightly puffed and golden.

Switch off the oven and open the door halfway. Leave like this for 10 minutes before removing the *clafoutis*. Take out of the roasting tin, allow to cool to lukewarm, sprinkle with a little more sifted icing sugar and serve with lightly sweetened whipped cream, perhaps flavoured with a trickle of pear *eau de vie*.

Baked Quinces ⁞ serves 4

The original recipe for this dish – from Joyce Molyneux's *Carved Angel Cookery Book* – uses honey. Well, you can also if you *really* wish to, but I prefer to add a split vanilla pod, bay leaves and a little more sugar. For best results when baking quinces, use a heavy lidded cast-iron pot – Le Creuset, for example – of a size that will accommodate the fruit snugly.

4 tbsp golden caster sugar
  (or honey)
8 tbsp water
1 vanilla pod, split lengthways

4 ripe, unblemished yellow quinces, well washed, left whole and not peeled
2 small bay leaves, fresh if possible

Preheat the oven to 350°F/180°C/gas mark 4.

Melt together the sugar or honey and the water and add the vanilla pod. Bring to a simmer and put in the quinces and the bay leaves. Put the lid on and bake in the oven for 45 minutes to 1 hour. The flesh will be a lovely shade of pink and the texture soft, though still a little granular. Eat warm.

Baked quinces are lovely served just like this, but eaten with a properly made vanilla custard they are transformed into luxury class.

For the custard:
300ml milk
½ vanilla pod, split lengthways

4 egg yolks
75g caster sugar
75ml double cream

Heat the milk and the vanilla pod in a heavy-bottomed saucepan. Remove from the stove and whisk for a few seconds to release the vanilla seeds into the milk. Leave to infuse for 10 minutes and remove the vanilla pod (wash and keep for reuse). Briefly beat together the egg yolks and sugar and strain the warm milk over them, whisking as you go. Return to the saucepan and cook over a very low heat (with a heat-diffuser pad if possible) until limpid and lightly thickened. Some say it should coat the back of a wooden spoon, but I don't go along with this theory; it should be taken further than this, almost until there is the odd simmering blip on the surface. When you think it is ready, add the cream, give a final vigorous whisk to amalgamate and pour into a warm jug.

Note: If you are unlucky enough to split the custard, then give it a quick blast in a liquidizer.

Ginger Queen of Puddings ‡ serves 4

It was my good friend Martin Owen who inspired this dish, by doing a version of Queen of Puddings using marmalade instead of jam. Martin is a very good cook and is able, unlike me, to make three pheasants feed 10 or 12 people – and there are usually seconds too. But I suspect, possibly, that when he thought of that marmalade pudding, even he didn't reckon that only a few spoonfuls of jam left in an old jar in the cupboard would have been enough for a Queen of Puddings. So he used marmalade instead. Well, I hope that was how it happened – it is certainly the way the following, equally delicious version, came my way.

When I scrabbled through *my* store cupboard, all I could find was some ginger marmalade, which is nice, but not exactly blessed with that lovely burnt orange flavour. Ginger marmalade is more of an excuse for getting ginger onto buttered toast just because you happen to really like ginger a lot. But when I remembered that I had a bit of fresh ginger sitting in the fridge (I always do, as it happens), I realized that here could be the answer to something really quite special. And when I also recalled a half-used jar of stem ginger in the cupboard (OK, there is always some of that there too), that put the clincher on it. Ginger Queen of Puddings it was to be.

300 ml milk
grated rind of 1 lemon
4 globes stem ginger, diced
2 tbsp syrup from the ginger jar
a pinch of salt

50g fresh white breadcrumbs
2 eggs, separated
a smear of softened butter
3 tbsp ginger marmalade
65g caster sugar

Warm the milk with the lemon rind, remove from the heat, cover and leave to infuse for 30 minutes. Preheat the oven to 350°F/180°C/gas mark 4. Add the stem ginger, ginger syrup, salt, breadcrumbs and egg yolks to the milk and mix together thoroughly. Lightly butter a baking dish and pour in the mixture. Leave for 15 minutes to allow the crumbs to swell.

Bake in the oven for 20–25 minutes or until set and firm to the touch. Leave to rest for 10 minutes. Meanwhile, beat the egg whites until stiff, then start to add 50g of the caster sugar in a thin stream. Continue beating until thick and glossy. Spoon the ginger marmalade over the bready sponge, covering the whole surface, and then pile the meringue on top. Shape with the back of a spoon into soft peaks and sprinkle with the remaining sugar. Return the pudding to the oven for about 7–10 minutes, or until pale golden and the surface crusted. Leave to cool until lukewarm. Serve with very cold pouring cream, sweetened with a little more ginger syrup.

Caramelized Pear Condé   serves 4

Here we have a traditional rice pudding that is topped with fruit; pears in this case, though peaches are fine too. I happen to love tinned pears and peaches. In fact one of my favourite snacks is a bowl of either of these with plenty of Carnation milk poured over – and it is important here that both the fruit and milk are cold from the fridge. The *condé* should be served warm, but is also good with ice-cold Carnation poured over, creating an altogether different sensation. You can use fresh double cream if you are feeling chaste.

50g butter
50g caster sugar
100g round-grain rice
1 litre milk
1 vanilla pod, split lengthways

150ml double cream
a pinch of salt
4 pear (or peach) halves
½ tbsp icing sugar

Preheat the oven to 275°F/130°C/gas mark 1.

Melt the butter in a flameproof casserole and add the sugar and rice. Stir around and heat gently until it turns a bit sticky. Continue stirring until the rice looks puffy and has started to turn pale golden. Add the milk, which will seethe, turning the rice/butter/sugar mixture into lumps. Fear not. Feel around with a wooden spoon and disperse the lumps, because as the milk heats it will dissolve them. Scrape the vanilla pod of its seeds and add these to the milk (put the emptied pod into a pot of caster sugar for later use). Add the cream and salt, and bring to the boil. Place in the oven and cook for 3–4 hours, or until just starting to set, but still slightly liquid-looking. Leave the pudding to cool to lukewarm, when it will finish cooking in its own heat, and set. Preheat an overhead grill to its highest setting.

Drain the pears or peaches from their syrup and pat dry with paper towels. Slice them very thinly and neatly arrange them over the surface of the pudding. Sieve the icing sugar over the surface and put under the grill. Allow to gently caramelize and blister somewhat. Remove when suitably burnished and serve after about 5 minutes' resting time.

Blackcurrant Jelly and Honey Madeleines ‡ serves 6

This particular jelly has been on and off the menu at Bibendum since we opened the restaurant. However, its first outing was on the menu at the slightly more diminutive Hilaire, fifteen years ago, where I first caused a bit of a ripple in South Ken with such things as saffron mashed potato and grilled aubergine with pesto. Exciting days! The fruit jelly has truly remained everyone's favourite, and is gorgeous when served with freshly made warm madeleines and lightly sweetened whipped cream.

500g fresh blackcurrants
  (it can be very successfully made
  with frozen too)
225g sugar
300ml water
4 leaves gelatine
150ml port
2 tbsp crème de cassis

For the honey madeleines:
You will need a madeleine baking tray with the traditional indentations for these little sponges. Good kitchen shops stock them. One tray usually has six indentations.
100g butter
200g caster sugar
50g plain flour, sieved
50g ground almonds
3 egg whites
1 tbsp honey
a little melted butter and some flour, for lining the madeleine tins

Remove the blackcurrants from their stalks, but there is no need to top and tail them. Put into a stainless-steel or enamelled pan, together with the sugar and the water. Bring to the boil and simmer very gently, covered, for 10 minutes. Then tip into a sieve suspended over a bowl. Leave to drain and drip for a couple of hours. Don't be tempted to force the syrup through the sieve, as pressing it too much will cause the jelly to become cloudy. Discard the pulp, or eat it as jam – although it can be a bit dry and flavourless.

Soak the gelatine in cold water for a few minutes until soft and soggy. Gently warm the drained syrup and dissolve the gelatine in it. Add the port and cassis and stir in well. Line the base of 6 ramekins with circles of wetted greaseproof paper. Pour in the jelly and place in the fridge to set for at least 6 hours, or preferably overnight.

To make the madeleines, melt the 100g butter until it turns pale, golden brown. Pour into a metal bowl to cool. Mix together the sugar, flour and almonds in another bowl. Beat the egg whites with a whisk until light and spumous. Add the sugar/flour/almond mixture and thoroughly fold in. Now stir in the honey and browned butter.

Brush the indentations with the melted butter and then dust with flour. Tap out any excess flour. Pour about 1 tbsp of the mixture into each indentation; they must be filled to the brim. Put in the fridge for 1 hour and preheat the oven to 375°F/190°C/gas mark 5.

Bake in the oven for 15 minutes, or until golden, puffed up and firm to the touch. Leave to cool in their tins for a few moments, then lift out. Try and serve them warm with the jellies; the contrast is most agreeable.

Stewed Rhubarb and Custard ⁑ serves 4–6

The most important thing to remember when cooking rhubarb is not to add any water at all, as the rhubarb simply stews in its own abundant juices. The flavour of orange has a fine affinity with rhubarb, so too does ginger.

The custard recipe will, perhaps, make more than you need. Oh yeah?

700g young, pink rhubarb
grated rind of 2 oranges
175g caster sugar
5cm piece of fresh ginger, peeled and
   thickly sliced

For the custard:
500ml milk
1 vanilla pod, split lengthways
6 egg yolks
100g caster sugar

Pre-heat the oven to 325°F/160°C/gas mark 3.

Peel any parts of the rhubarb you might think are tough and stringy. Cut up into 4cm lengths, on the diagonal. Put into a stove-top to oven dish and put onto a low heat (this is just to get the dish hot for the oven). Stir the orange rind into the sugar in a bowl until it is thoroughly mixed together and strew evenly over the rhubarb. Put the lid on and place in the oven for 20 minutes. Have a look now and give the pot a brief shake about; try not to stir as this can break up the rhubarb. You will notice that some juice has already started to exude, but it will need another 15 minutes or so to be thoroughly cooked through. Remove from the oven, take off the lid and allow to cool. Remove the lumps of ginger and serve at room temperature with the custard.

To make the custard, heat the milk with the vanilla pod in a heavy bottomed saucepan. Remove from the stove and whisk for a few seconds to release the vanilla seeds into the milk. Briefly beat together the egg yolks and sugar and strain over the hot milk, whisking as you go. Return to the saucepan and cook over a very low heat (with a heat diffuser if possible) until limpid and lightly thickened. Some say it should coat the back of a wooden spoon, but I don't go along with this theory; it should be taken further than this, almost until there is the odd simmering blip on the surface. When you think it is ready, give a final vigorous whisk to amalgamate and pour into a warm jug.

Note: If you are unlucky enough to split the custard, a blast in the liquidizer will rescue it.

Raspberry Crème Brûlée – without the Brûlée ⚕ serves 4–5

The idea for this rich little number came to me when I wanted to make a crème brûlée but did not have access to a grill. In a way, I find it a nicer dish than crème brûlée made with raspberries lurking at the bottom of the dish, buried under the custard. I always think they disturb the smoothness of the thing, and appear as an unwanted surprise. Raspberries are just the tops on this little pot of yellow eggy cream.

600ml double cream
1 vanilla pod, split lengthways
4 large egg yolks

2 tbsp caster sugar
250g raspberries
about 1 tbsp sieved icing sugar

Heat the cream with the vanilla pod in a heavy-based saucepan, until hot but not boiling. Whisk thoroughly for a few seconds to disperse the seeds from the vanilla pod, cover and leave to infuse for 30 minutes. Meanwhile, gently whisk together the egg yolks and sugar. Remove the vanilla pod from the cream, shake well, lightly rinse and store in some sugar if you like – or – something I have recently taken to in a big way – bury them in with your coffee beans; the subtle flavour, once brewed, is delightful.

Pour the warm cream over the egg yolks and sugar and whisk together. Return to the pan and cook very gently over a low heat, stirring with a wooden spoon. Everybody (well *almost* everybody) tells you to cook the custard until it coats the back of a wooden spoon. I think this is mislead-ing, as the mixture almost coats the spoon from the start, resulting in an insufficiently cooked custard that won't set. I find – and it becomes easier and less risky with practice – that one can almost allow the occasional boiling blip (and I mean occasional!) to form on the surface, followed by vigorous whisking to disperse them back into the less hot parts of the custard. Finally, the consistency should be one of cold tinned Heinz tomato soup, which, as everyone knows, coats the back of a wooden spoon superbly well – and is not the daft analogy it sounds.

When you feel that the custard is ready, pour it either into one large shallow dish or if you are in the neat and tidy dinner party mood into generous-sized individual ramekins and chill well for at least 4 hours.

Note: The mixture should not be much higher than two-thirds up the sides of whichever container you are using, so as to make room for the raspberries. Carefully pile the raspberries on top and dust generously with the icing sugar. Serve straightaway.

Coffee Granita ⚜ serves 4

The very best coffee granita I have yet eaten was at Tre Scalini, on the Piazza Navona, in Rome. It was possibly the hottest day of July 1996, and that spectacular, deeply cooling glass of granita – even though it was clad with a collar of whipped cream – welcomely refreshed the rigours of my morning's culture.

600 ml very strong coffee   *120g caster sugar*
(espresso is best)

Chill a shallow metal tray in the freezer in advance.

While the coffee is still hot whisk in the sugar until dissolved. Cool completely and then pour into the chilled tray. Place in the freezer for about an hour and then have a look. What you are looking for is ice crystals forming around the edge of the tray (completely opposite to ice cream or sorbets, as here the ice crystals are the essential charm of the thing). Once the crystals have reached about 5–7 cm towards the middle of the tray, gently lift them with a fork into the not-so-frozen coffee. Return to the freezer. Have another look in about 30 minutes and repeat this forking about.

Continue this procedure until all the mixture has formed crystals; it may take up to 2 hours or so. Once made, tip into a suitable lidded plastic container and store in the freezer until ready to use. The granita will keep its granular texture for several days, but after that the granita starts to firm up into a block. However, it is simple to start again by just melting the coffee over heat and going through the motions once more. To serve the granita, pile into tall glasses and top with a large spoonful of *crème Chantilly* (see page 182).

Hazelnut Meringue Cake ‡ serves 6

I have never been great at making cakes. This one, however, has never been too much trouble. It turns out as a sort of marshmallow meringue thing, slightly chewy and not terribly nice to look at actually. However, once sandwiched together with the whipped cream and raspberries, it comes together like bananas and custard.

It is well worth grinding your own hazelnuts here, which results in a finer-flavoured cake. Try to buy them ready skinned, dry-roast for a few minutes in a moderately hot oven and then grind up in a food processor or coffee grinder.

4 large egg whites
a pinch of salt
225g + 1 tbsp caster sugar
2–3 drops pure vanilla
 extract

½ tsp white spirit vinegar or cider
 vinegar
100g ground hazelnuts (sifted)
300ml double cream
350g raspberries

Butter and flour two 20 cm × 4 cm loose-bottomed cake tins and line each base with a circle of baking parchment. Preheat the oven to 375°F/190°C/gas mark 5.

Whisk the egg whites until they form soft peaks, then whisk the 225 g of sugar 1 tbsp at a time. Once the mixture is glossy and stiff, whisk in the vanilla and vinegar and then fold in the ground hazelnuts. Equally fill the two prepared tins with the meringue mixture and smooth the tops with a metal spoon dipped in hot water. Bake for about 35–40 minutes until the top is blotchy-golden and crisp. Remove and allow to cool for a few minutes before removing from the tins (they do tend to sink a little, so don't worry). Turn out onto a cooling rack and remove the parchment while still warm.

Once the cakes are completely cold, whip the cream with the remaining sugar until just holding peaks. Spread onto the surface of one of the cakes and then evenly pile on the raspberries. Carefully press the other cake on top. Leave to settle for at least an hour, as it will then be easier to cut.

Finishing touches and variations: swirls of extra whipped cream around the top surface and decorated with more raspberries; sifted icing sugar; a purée of raspberries to serve as a sauce; raspberry *eau de vie* added to the whipped cream or into a sauce.

Lemon Posset   ‡   enough to fill 8–10 ramekins

I first came across this remarkable little dessert whilst enjoying the closing moments of a delicious lunch cooked by one Lucy Crabb, when she was cooking in a country restaurant in Suffolk.

Lucy was one amongst the first team of a group of very special chefs who started up Bibendum with me in 1987. She is a remarkably natural cook, has since become a close friend and possesses one of the dirtiest laughs I know.

I cannot remember the origins of this posset, but it remains one of the easiest desserts it is possible to make.

Left: **Hazelnut Meringue Cake**

1 litre double cream   juice of 4 lemons
275g caster sugar

Bring the cream and sugar to the boil in a large pan; this is important, to
allow for the expansion of the cream as it boils – and it must boil for
exactly 3 minutes. Take off the heat and whisk in the lemon juice. Strain
through a fine sieve into a bowl and then ladle into the ramekins. Chill
for at least 4 hours before serving.

Brandy Alexander Ice Cream   ‡   serves 4

The Groucho Club, in London's Soho, makes a very good Brandy
Alexander. It is a favourite – albeit slightly tarty – late-night cocktail of
mine, fashioned from cognac, Kalhua (chocolate liqueur) and cream,
shaken over ice, strained into a chilled glass and dusted with nutmeg. I
always think (usually after about the third glass), that it would make a
wonderful ice cream. Curiously, the following morning, I never recall this
wizard idea. That is, until now.

5 medium egg yolks   2 tbsp good cognac
90g caster sugar   3 tbsp Kalhua
a generous grating of nutmeg   150ml double cream

In a roomy bowl, over a pan of gently simmering water, beat the egg
yolks, sugar and nutmeg together until very thick and light. Add the
cognac and Kalhua and continue beating until the consistency is billowy,
yet still continuing to thicken. Remove from the heat and continue beating until the mixture has cooled down. Whip the cream until only loosely
thick and fold carefully into the egg mixture. Spoon into small wine
glasses, leaving a 1cm gap at the top. Seal with a small piece of clingfilm
and place in the freezer for at least 6 hours, or overnight.

Remove the glasses to the fridge for 20 minutes before you wish to eat
the ice cream. Lift off the clingfilm, pour a spoonful of double cream over
each serving and grate a little more nutmeg on top.

Note: An electric hand whisk will ease the making of this ice cream, although hand whisking with a fine balloon whisk will produce a finer texture.

Recipe Index

General Index